GERARD LEES

THANKFUL
and not so
THANKFUL

HOW THE GREAT WAR CHANGED
THREE ENGLISH VILLAGES FOREVER

GERARD LEES

THANKFUL
and not so
THANKFUL

HOW THE GREAT WAR CHANGED
THREE ENGLISH VILLAGES FOREVER

MEREO
Cirencester

Mereo Books

1A The Wool Market Dyer Street Cirencester Gloucestershire GL7 2PR
An imprint of Memoirs Publishing www.mereobooks.com

Thankful and not so thankful: 978-1-86151-271-0

First published in Great Britain in 2014
by Mereo Books, an imprint of Memoirs Publishing

Copyright ©2014

Gerard Lees has asserted his right under the Copyright Designs and Patents
Act 1988 to be identified as the author of this work.

A CIP catalogue record for this book is available from the British Library.

The address for Memoirs Publishing Group Limited can be found at
www.memoirspublishing.com

The Memoirs Publishing Group Ltd Reg. No. 7834348

The Memoirs Publishing Group supports both The Forest Stewardship Council® (FSC®) and
the PEFC® leading international forest-certification organisations. Our books carrying both the
FSC label and the PEFC® and are printed on FSC®-certified paper. FSC® is the only
forest-certification scheme supported by the leading environmental organisations including
Greenpeace. Our paper procurement policy can be found at
www.memoirspublishing.com/environment

Typeset in 11/15pt Bembo
by Wiltshire Associates Publisher Services Ltd. Printed and bound in Great Britain by
Printondemand-Worldwide, Peterborough PE2 6XD

ACKNOWLEDGEMENTS

The writing of this book proved to be a journey which was arduous and rewarding in fairly equal proportions. I met or communicated with many helpful people along the way, from residents of the villages to institutions in Canada, New Zealand and Australia, as well as in the UK. All were generous with their time and in many cases hospitable in welcoming me into their homes. I am grateful to them all, and hope I have reciprocated by doing justice to the historical fabric and the people interwoven into it.

I owe a debt to my family, and to my wife, Joanne, for showing unwavering support throughout. She was responsible for the idea of the book, with the comment as we looked at the scroll in St John's, Arkholme that "You'd better write about this". My son and daughter, Tim and Emily, have shown immense patience throughout, especially when rescuing me when I had saved a fact, testimony or picture in totally the wrong place on the laptop. My friend of over forty years, Steve Kay, now resident in the United States, has, as usual, displayed unflagging encouragement, as well as doing a bit of informal proofreading when he really could have claimed pressure of work not to. Thanks to all.

Finally, this book would not have been written – or would have taken as long to write as the Great War lasted - without the input of Jan Tivey. Genealogist extraordinaire, she was only an email away on so many occasions and showed a remarkable and continuing belief in me and in the project.

I now hope I have done justice to the people of three villages in England, who in so many ways epitomised the efforts of the whole of Britain in the years from 1914 to 1918 and after.

Gerard Lees, July 2014 | statist@blueyonder.co.uk

CHAPTER ONE

HOW IT STARTED

'Home wasn't a set house, or a single town on a map. It was wherever the people who loved you were, whenever you were together. Not a place, but a moment, and then another' - Sarah Dressen

My wife and I had holidayed at the resort of Pine Lake a couple of times before. A good friend has a cabin there and it is perfect for us. Just north east of Carnforth, it is close to the beautiful and sometimes scary Morecambe Bay and is a stopping point on the way to the Lake District and a gateway to one of Britain's prettiest secrets, the Trough of Bowland.

This March day we had decided – on a host of recommendations – to visit Kirkby Lonsdale, about a dozen miles away. We took the main A road rather than the motorway, planning a stop for drinks and snacks at, hopefully, a village shop on the way.

After about five miles of travel we came across a sign. It said 'Arkholme with Cawood', which seemed to fit the bill. My wife was driving and I hopped out at what appeared to be the centre; a Methodist chapel. When we do this sort of thing, whoever's driving tends to sort out the food and drink while the other wanders around for an exploration.

As we tended to do in places we didn't know, we arranged to meet at the war memorial – usually central or in the parish churchyard. I'd had an interest in World War One since we'd moved to a new house when I was fifteen and met my next door neighbour Wilfred Rostron. Wilf, a WW1 'Tommy', had told me stories of attacking at dawn, of mates lost and of heroes and idiots. This was augmented with a study of history at university and a few visits to France and Belgium.

I came to a junction with the Bay Horse pub on one side and on the other side a lane to the right with a sign indicating a church. I walked further on and passed a really splendid village hall; clearly the subject of some love, affection and pride, it was bedecked by flowers on this sunny spring day. About half a mile further on the road crossed over a railway line; the old station was there and someone had clearly put a lot of time, work and effort into revamping and modernising it into a spectacular home. The road disappeared into the countryside and I turned back.

About now I should have been meeting up with my better half at the memorial. Back at the junction, where these are usually sited, there was no sign. I spotted the 'CHURCH' sign again and made my way along the road, passing pretty whitewashed cottages on the road towards what turned out to be St John the Baptist's. I used my mobile to tell her where I was going; she was already inside the church.

It was picture postcard. Backed up to what looked like a man-made mound of grass (it turned out to be a Norman motte or defensive hill) it sat on the northern bank of the Lune, one of the prettiest rivers in England – and that's according to Wordsworth, Turner and Ruskin, not bad judges.

I looked for the memorial, but all I could find was what looked like a square sandstone foundation, or a base for something much older than the 1920s.

My wife emerged from the church.

'So, where's the memorial?' I asked.

'There isn't one.'

'What, a place like this can't be bothered to put one up?'

'No. Go into the church. It tells you. They haven't got one because all but one of them got back alive, as far as I can make out. There's a plaque on the back wall with a roll of honour of all their names.'

'All got back from the war? Unbelievable.'

'Both wars. Apart from one man, I think.'

'Both? That's impossible.'

And there the quest started. The scroll or plaque was beautifully written on parchment-like paper, inside a wood and glass case. It was about two feet long by eighteen inches across, with two rows of names and a regiment or battalion after each name. We took photographs of it and then the inside and grounds of the church,

The scroll in St John the Baptist's church at Arkholme

and resumed our trip to Kirkby Lonsdale.

Back in the cabin at Pine Lake I googled 'Places with no War Memorial.' The words 'Thankful Village' came up. 'Thankful Villages: the places where everyone came back.' It was a BBC report by Jon Kay from Armistice Day, 2011. Now I understood.

The next entry was a Wikipedia report naming fifty-one places, and also referring to them as 'Blessed

Villages'. Arkholme was in there with its neighbour Nether Kellet. Both then had a '(D) The Returners' Scroll' behind their names – indicating a Doubly Thankful Village, whatever that was. There were thirteen of those. Then followed a report by someone I was familiar with, Tom Morgan, who runs a website called 'Hellfire Corner' (so named after a junction on the Menin Road outside Ypres) and then an article by Historic UK. I paraphrase from the latter.

The term 'Thankful Village' was first used by the British writer and journalist Arthur Mee in his King's England, a guide to the English counties, in the 1930s. A Thankful Village was said to be one which lost no men in the Great War, as all those who had left to serve King and Country came home again. For instance, he writes about Catwick in the Yorkshire East Riding: 'Thirty men went from Catwick to the Great War and thirty came back, though one left an arm behind'. I read on and discovered that, incredibly, Arkholme claimed fifty-nine 'Returners', men who went to war and got back alive. It was also said that such villages had no war memorials, although some had monuments, usually in the church, in gratitude for their good fortune.

Among the sixteen thousand villages in England, Arthur Mee estimated that there were at most thirty-two designated as Thankful, although he could only positively identify twenty-four. The count increased to forty-one, now upgraded to fifty-three after research by Morgan and his colleagues Norman Thorpe and Rod Morris.

Doubly Thankful Villages, where all who went away to serve and returned alive in both wars, were numbered on Wikipedia at thirteen, though other testimony suggests Colwinston in Wales as one more. Arkholme and Nether Kellet were both listed as 'Doubly Thankful'.

A couple of weeks later, on a beautiful late spring day, we visited St John the Baptist's again. Down the country lane, past the whitewashed Reading Room on the left and the Rose Cottage on the other side, we walked until we met the path to the Ferryman's Cottage. Opposite is the short lane to the church and behind, the River Lune, shallow and languid on this gentle afternoon. Inside, on the south wall, was the plaque with the fifty-nine names of Returners of the First War and the sixteen men and two women who did the same in the Second. But there was an anomaly: on the west wall was a stone rectangle with an inscription on it. So if this man left Arkholme to go to war and didn't come back, the village wasn't a Doubly Thankful one.

The following Friday, Lancaster University, via librarian Liz Hartley (who by chance lives in Arkholme), opened its archives and let me see the *Lancaster Observer* and *Morecambe Guardian* newspapers from 1941 and 1942. There, at the bottom of page 4 in the Christmas Eve edition was a report of a missing seaman, Harold Edward Newby. It was entitled ARKHOLME. He was Leading Stoker on HMS *Repulse*, sunk off Pahong, north of Singapore, by

Report from the *Lancaster Observer and Morecambe Guardian*, 1941

the Japanese when, with the *Prince of Wales*, it was trying to resist the invasion of Malaysia. From a crew of one thousand one hundred and eighty-one sailors, five hundred and thirteen perished. Harold was one of them. The report said he was 'not reported as a survivor'.

In March 1941, Harold had married a Nellie Metcalfe, of Arkholme, in St John the Baptist's, where the Roll of Honour plaque is displayed, and where the tribute to him would sadly be placed. After his death, she got married again in June, 1944 - to his younger brother, Ernest. They had two boys, Thomas William, in 1945, and Harold Peter, in 1946. Nellie is, with one other woman, named on the plaque in St John's as having survived the war after service in the WRAF. She died in 1998 aged eighty-one, and her husband Ernie in 2008 aged eighty-seven.

The first son, Tom, is alive and well and living in in Carnforth; his younger brother Peter has lived in Canada for forty years. Ernie was on another ship which was in the vicinity and was due to meet up with his older brother Harold, in Singapore some time in December 1941 (were they trying for a Christmas get together?). Then the tragedy occurred. So the village of Arkholme didn't classify as a Doubly Thankful one.

Just over six miles to the south west is a neighbour that did. Nether Kellet sent twenty-one of its men to the First War and then sixteen – some the sons of the twenty-one – to the second, and got them all back. This does make it Doubly Thankful, one of just over a dozen villages in England that can be so described. Nearly in between is Over Kellet; there, in the middle of two greens, is a feature seen in over a hundred thousand towns, villages and cities in Britain – the war memorial. On it are ten names from the First War and two from the Second.

These three villages, less than ten miles apart, characterise the years around the First World War. The people who were born in them, lived in them, left them and perished or returned, summarise British society and its response to the European War(s). Their story is one of three north Lancashire villages, but it is more, much more than that. Two of the villages are unusual in that they had a full complement of survivors who had fought abroad, from the present Iraq to France and Belgium. Once that is said, they are typical of almost any three British villages in the years 1914 to 1918. They were Britain's Great War.

In Arkholme and Nether Kellet the soldiers must surely have been in one or two regiments that were in quiet areas of some peaceful part of the war. And the Over Kellet men must, presumably, have been unlucky.

Well, not quite.

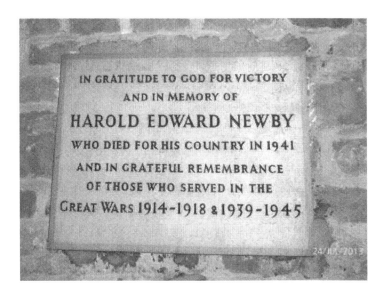

Tribute to Harold Newby inside St John's

CHAPTER TWO

THE VILLAGES

'Few things are more pleasant than a village graced with a good church, a good priest and a good pub' - John Hillaby

'The sun does not forget a village just because it is small' - African proverb

In 1911, three years before the assassination of Archduke Franz Ferdinand and the resultant First World War, a census was taken in Britain. In that year the people would have been interested in the developments in road and air travel; in India the first delivery of mail from one town to another took place when Henri Pequet flew from Allahabad to Naini. Transport was still mainly by horse in one form or another, though by 1911, Rolls Royce, Morris, Vauxhall and Ford were all producing cars in the UK. Most British towns had electric street lights. The May newspapers carried the news of the launch of an unprecedentedly huge passenger ship called the *Titanic*. The census was in April and on the night of its process a certain Emily Davison locked herself in a room in the House of Commons to legitimately register as a resident. Two years later she died under the hooves of the King's horse at the Epsom Derby. That king, George V, was crowned at Westminster in midsummer 1911, a summer that broke all previous records for heat and aridity.

After the war, that conflict was blamed for many social and economic difficulties. Certainly the country was debt-ridden, but there had been strife before the war, as exemplified by the nearly fifteen hundred strikes that took place in 1913. Irish Home Rule was at the top of the pre-war political agenda, women wanted the vote as described above and inequalities of wealth were huge. The child death rate was a hundred and twenty-seven per one thousand live births; now it's under five, and average life expectancy was around fifty for men and a few years more for women. Over twenty-five per cent of the population were living in poverty, of which fifteen per cent were living on a subsistence level – they could afford only the basics of food, clothing and fuel. The other ten per cent were below this. Most people had tough lives, though that adjective is of course a subjective one.

I give you three quotes from Max Arthur's *Lost Voices of The Edwardians* to lend a flavour of pre-war Britain:

'I was born in Morecambe in April 1895 and my father was a tailor. When I was six or seven I remember eating one of my father's tomatoes from his window box, and he got hold of me and held me under a cold water tap. Not long after that he did a bunk. We understood he joined the Black Watch Regiment but were never sure. Of course there was no Social Security then and we were soon absolutely broke, so my mother put us on a tram to Lancaster and we all went into the workhouse. We didn't live as a family. The food was very rough and we didn't get enough. Every Saturday they used to give us a cup of Epsom salts. You can guess where we spent the Sunday. - Joe Armstrong

'If we didn't go to Goulston Street Baths we'd bath in this big zinc bath one after the other in the same water. By the time we was finished, it was like ink.' - Minnie Lane

'All the world is changing at once' - Winston Churchill

The settlements of Arkholme, Over Kellet and Nether Kellet provide the three points of a very flat triangle, the longest side from Arkholme to Nether Kellet being about six miles long. Taking in Over Kellet would add only a mile to the journey. Arkholme is arguably the prettiest of the villages, as in the summer months it has a slow, languid section of the River Lune at its south-eastern corner. It is overlooked by the aforementioned honey-coloured church of St John The Baptist, its adjacent man-made hill and the ferryman's cottage. From the main crossroad that hosts the village shop/post office and the Bay Horse pub, the road splits north to a small housing development and south east to the church and river. Carry on in the direction of Kirkby Lonsdale and you pass the prize-winning village hall and further on a railway bridge and the old station and stationmaster's house. The latter has been wonderfully preserved and developed at the same time by Jim Bowen of The Comedians and Bullseye fame; after finishing a degree at Lancaster University Jim obviously and understandably developed a great affection for this part of the world, becoming a deputy headmaster in Caton near the river Lune before embarking on his show business career. The vicar of St John's lives there now. The trains don't stop any more but hurry on to Melling, Yorkshire and beyond.

Two other notable – and totally appropriate - names for jobs in 1911 were the policeman Harold Gilbody (it would have almost been nice to be arrested by a copper called Harold Gilbody) and the vicar of St John's, the Rev W Shepherd. Did he avoid Psalm 23 which begins: 'The Lord is my shepherd'?

The village developed a mini industry of basket making to fill the market demand of agriculture and the Morecambe Bay shrimp

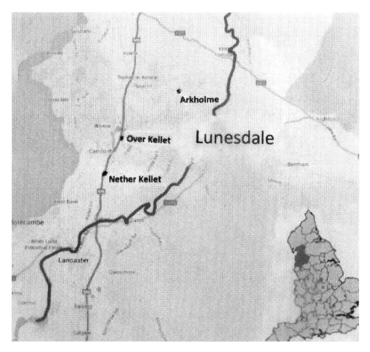

The locations of the three Thankful Villages in North Lancashire

industry, with the Ireland family (of whom more later) being its best known proponent. Being near the main western highway on the way to Scotland, it saw more than one incursion; in the seventies, Richard Haston found a semi-fossilised musket in the stream of his farm. Possibly ditched by a retreating Jacobite in 1745, it sits on a high shelf of his and his wife Joan's neat cottage in nearby Hornby.

Back through the village towards Over and Nether Kellet and Lancaster are the gates to Storrs Hall, for all intents and purposes the Lord of the Manor's place. An original building and land was purchased by Francis Fenwick Pearson in the 1840s, but it was demolished and the Gothic structure we see now built in its stead. The Pearsons were a well-known Westmorland and then Lancashire family of military men and solicitors and it was a subsequent descendant, again Francis Fenwick, who inherited the Hall in 1910. His name is on the Arkholme church plaque. The Booth family who originated from Rochdale were tenants, as were the Parkers and Cyril Rivett. Frank Booth has a World War One history all of his own, which is explored in Chapter Four.

Storrs Hall

John and Stephen Parker were the sons of James and Hannah, the former being the gamekeeper for the Pearsons, and lived in Storrs cottage. John, aged thirty-four when war broke out, joined the Liverpool Scottish, and his brother, after emigrating to Canada, was in the British Columbia Horse at the outbreak of the conflict in August, 1914, but was discharged with defective eyesight and varicose veins, not great attributes for a potential soldier. Cyril Rivett, who was a boarder at the cottage with them, was the Pearson's chauffeur and carried on using these skills in the army. He had moved up from Plymouth to take the job as a driver – not everyone could do that in the first years of the twentieth century.

He was conscripted in 1916 and joined the Army Service Corps as a mechanic. He had married Jessica, from Hawes in west Yorkshire, in 1912; she was six months pregnant at the time. After the war they moved to Penzance where he became a coach driver.

When they left to fight in the tragedy of the First War, however, Cyril and John Parker fitted into the constraints of the social strata of the day. They were automatically, because of their occupations, designated as privates. It would be a later cultural change in opportunities and expectations and the free education of the sixties with its desire from universities for attested levels of intelligence that the abilities of the working class and the subsequent institution of some form of meritocracy took place and with it the accompanying benefits to society.

At the outbreak of war in 1914, the village is recorded as housing three hundred and nineteen people with a few more men than women; this is an assumption, as some women in the country refused to participate as a protest at not having the vote. The latter was to be partially awarded seven years later, mainly as a result of the war, but not fully and on not on equal terms to men for another seventeen years.

Called Nether to distinguish it from its higher neighbour (in altitude, not in cultural or sociological terms) Over Kellet, the village of Nether Kellet just lacks a lake, canal or river to give it a description of 'lovely' or 'picture postcard'. 'Kellet' is an old word in the north of England for spring – the water type, not the season. Located a mile inland from the aptly named Bolton-le-Sands, it sits in rolling limestone hills with views over Morecambe Bay. Driving in from Arkholme, it is clearly a comfortable village to live in, the main road bending to the left after the small, squat, bell-topped church of St Mark's. A little further on is the village shop, and then playing fields stretch out for a couple of hundred yards. Ironically, the first thing that strikes you as you go through the village is that you could easily be driving through a settlement in rural France or Belgium, which is where twenty-one of the villagers were headed in the second decade of the twentieth century; unfortunately they weren't holidaying. The road then runs past the solid walls of the backs of farms; it is punctuated by well-kept flower-basketed houses, built predominantly of the grey/honey biscuit limestone quarried just a few hundred yards away.

Nether Kellet, St Mark's bottom right

Returners' scroll, Nether Kellet

The name of the pub on the main road, the Limeburner Arms, gives away a little of the village's industrial character as it would have been in the years just prior to the First World War. A browse of the 1911 census gives a flavour of the way that the good people of Nether Kellet earned their living. Christopher Orr was an oil boilerman at the local lino works, Joseph Standon worked on the farms and Walter Jackson was a builder's labourer; much the type of jobs you might expect in a small rural community in a predominantly industrial county in Britain. Walter probably sweated through those hot months as he helped build and repair properties in the settlements east of Carnforth; little did he know he would be sweating in a totally different type of work before the next census was taken.

It was July when we visited. On the outside of the shop a rough glass case contained a variety of local information, including an A4 sheet with a list of names put there by an R Mace. This turned out to be Roger Mace, councillor for the villages of Nether Kellet, Over Kellet and Arkholme and regular helpful gent; the first of many the author would meet in the journey to discover, and hopefully honour the villages' Great War men and women. The list included fourteen men – and boys – who joined up during the years 1914 to 1918, who could be traced in the 1911 census. It also refers to another seven who could not.

We met the vicar's husband Nigel (now what would the guys of the second decade of the twentieth century have thought of that – vicar's husband?), who would let us into the church. Nigel is a very affable relocated Scouser – but aren't all relocated Scousers affable? The reason we wanted to get into the building was attached to the North West wall. A dark brown, oak-varnished plaque, it was obviously often polished and reflected the sunrays coming in from the window on the opposite side of the aisle, partially obscuring the last eight or nine names written on it in dark lettering. They read 'Bibby, Bradshaw, Crossley' … through 'Pollock, Robinson, and Standen to Horrocks, Moore and Stott'. Such simple letters, all making up a name, a life and an experience.

We took photos, thanked our host and made to leave. 'I'll show you the Peace Stone if you like,' Nigel offered. We walked past the shop and a row of houses on the left. The one nearest the centre was a 'Jubilee Cottage'. This would have been Jubilee Terrace in 1911, in which lived three future soldiers and returners, Christopher Orr, Walter Jackson and Joseph Standen. About eighty yards further on, a sharp right turn leads into the playing fields, and there is the Peace Stone. The inscription on it tells its own story:

This Tribute to a lasting peace was planted By T C Butler-Cole, Esq of Tunstall House and Mrs S T Whalen of this village at Nether Kellet Peace Celebrations To Commemorate the Cessation of Hostilities in the 2nd World War 3rd Sept 1939- 15th Aug 1945

The Peace Stone at Nether Kellet

The 'planted' refers to a tree; it originally overshadowed the Peace Stone which was moved from its first location and which may be moved again. The unusual part of the Stone's testimony is the reference to August. Most First World War memorials give its dates as 1914–1918. In fact, November 1918 saluted the Armistice and, of course, as it turned out, the real end of the war. Technically the peace was signed in the Versailles Hall of Mirrors in the summer of 1919, and thus the First World War ran from 1914–1919. Then again, because of the split of Germany into West and East in 1945, the Allies did not formally enter a peace arrangement with all of Germany until the unification in 1990! So the Second World War didn't fully and technically end until Japan's surrender; and that wasn't until the 2nd of September 1945.

Emperor Hirohito had given a recorded radio address across the Empire on August 15th. In the radio address, called the 'Jewel Voice Broadcast', he announced the surrender of Japan to the Allies. And that is why that date is on the Peace Stone.

Driving into Over Kellet from the north east, the first thing you experience is the fleeting, tantalising, and on a sunny day, beautiful, views of Morecambe Bay. The road then drops down into what seem to be two village greens. It's a historical place, or at least a place where history was written; William Farrer, who wrote the four volumes of the History of the County of Lancaster, was a resident. On the left is an ancient stone cross and the road that leads past the Eagle's Head and on towards the church of St Cuthbert's and the quarries. On the right is a truncated column on top of a four-foot high limestone base and is something not seen in Arkholme or Nether Kellet: the war memorial. The top does look as though it was once much higher, but it has been bisected or decapitated by a shell. It was built that way to represent unfinished

lives; on the northern side of the base are two names from the
Second War; on the southern side are ten from the First:

J ALEXANDER	A J GRAHAM
G LEE BOOKER	T HODGSON
F W BULLOUGH	J E ROBINSON
T EDWARDS	T TOWNSON
E EDWARDS	J WESTERN

The War Memorial, Over Kellet

Like the scrolls in the churches of Arkholme and Nether Kellet, these are letters put together to make a sound, a means of recognition, a piece of DNA, a journey. At the time I did not know that up the road from this memorial is another one in the cemetery of the aforementioned St Cuthbert's Parish Church. It has the same names. Another thing I was ignorant of was that in that burial place lies one of the men on the memorials who survived the fighting and succumbed to disease; well, a deadly virus, anyway. In the villages I was to discover heroism on a grand scale, villagers who returned from abroad to fight for their home country and women who risked their lives only a few miles away. I would discover pioneers in communications, prisoners of war and survivors of near-suicidal acts of valour. And I would meet some great people and find out more about one of England's loveliest areas; Lunesdale.

We had a pint of 'Lancaster Guzzler' underneath the single old tree in the garden of the Eagles Head. Was it, or a similar one, growing there in the second decade of the twentieth century? Did the Edwards have a leg-pull with each other there in the summer of 1914? Did G. Lee Booker go with his Dad there for his first pint? (No). Was J. E. Robinson a relative of the Nether Kellet Robinsons but not as fortunate in war? Who was Fred Bullough, and what did he do? And how many villagers managed to get back in one piece and emulate their neighbours in Nether Kellet and Arkholme?

CHAPTER THREE

ORDINARY HEROES: WALTER JACKSON AND GEORGE HARRISON

'Heroes are made by the paths they choose, not the powers they are graced with' - Brodi Ashton

Walter Jackson (pictured) was born in Nether Kellet a week or so before Christmas 1885. He was christened at Bolton-le-Sands, where his remains lie today. His story is in some respects typical of the hard times he lived in. He never knew his mother Agnes, as she, it is thought, was disowned by her parents on getting pregnant out of wedlock at the early age of sixteen years. She gave birth to Walter when she was seventeen.

This was something that Walter was bitter about all his life, and he thought his mother didn't want him. It's more likely that her family brought pressure to bear and she was sent away to live with relatives and not allowed to 'darken' the family home's doorstep again. Conversely, it might simply have been that she was given the chance by her parents to make a new life for herself.

Walter was brought up by his grandfather John Jackson and grandmother Ann, both of whom he spoke of very highly. His grandmother, who brought him up, was in fact his step-grandmother, but whether Walter knew this isn't known. Before Walter's age had reached double figures, his grandfather John was badly hurt when a rock fell on him at the quarry he partly owned and worked at. For a few years, Walter was then brought up by his grandfather John's brother Isaac and Isaac's wife, Jane. With no social security and only the workhouse for people to fall back on, John sold all his possessions, including a pocket watch which had been a present and which he treasured. He died prematurely, at the age of fifty-nine, in 1894.

Walter Jackson

Walter became a builder's labourer and by 1911 was living in Jubilee Terrace, Nether Kellet, with his wife Florence, whom he had married in 1905, and daughters Nancy and Nellie. Perhaps his grandfather's accident had put him off the family tradition of quarry work, but in any case he still chose a very physical way of making his living, in the building trade. Walter joined the army at the outbreak of war in 1914, and spent much of the following three years in training, being billeted in places of variable quality.

The latter end of 1916 saw the need for fresh troops in France/Belgium and his battalion was located to Kent. He had clearly shown natural leadership qualities and achieved the rank of Sergeant in February, 1917. The photograph highlights his proficiency and status as a sniper instructor.

On March 6th, the King's Own 2/5th battalion sailed from Southampton to Le Havre on the SS *Queen Alexandra* and the SS *Manchester Importer*. A thirty-nine hour train journey was endured, stopping at Montrelier–Bughy and Abbeville. The latter, poignantly, is on the Somme and hosted one of the biggest military hospitals on the Western Front. In February, 1917, it would have been full of those injured at the Somme. It now is the site of a huge military cemetery, containing both Allied and German fatalities.

By the next month Walter found himself near Fleurbaix, five or six miles to the south west of Armentières and three or four miles north of a place called Fromelles.

Fifty miles south of there, the battle of the Somme was in its third week. On the 18th and 19th of July there was a pause due to poor weather. General Horne, Commander of XV Corps opposite High Wood, wrote: 'The last few overcast days have prevented our air work, and the Hun has been able to place guns and bring up troops out of sight. There must be pauses in a great battle in order to arrange matters.'

A few miles away General Hubert de la Poer Gough, Commander of the Reserve Corps, summoned General Walker, the Australian Commander of 1st Division. He told him to attack Pozières, so far unbreakable and one of the strongest German positions on the Somme, standing on the Thiepval Ridge, 'at once'. Walker delayed to make assessments and then followed the order.

The village was taken on the 23rd and defended against a counter attack the following day. Disastrously for the Australian troops, their 2nd Division was then ordered by Gough to take Mouquet ('Mucky') Farm. The 1st Division had suffered over five thousand casualties, according to Wilson and Prior, and the troops were described by Sergeant E. J. Rule as being 'drawn and haggard and so dazed that they seemed to be walking in a dream'. The subsequent fighting and losses by the 1st/8th Warwickshires and the 7th East Surreys, as well as the Aussies, was brutal and overwhelming. The farm wasn't taken until 26th September. The Australians suffered a further eight thousand six hundred casualties and it is said that they never trusted British military leadership again.

Back at Fromelles, their compatriots, plus a British division, were on an equally fruitless venture.

In 2000, Robin Corfield self-published *Don't Forget Me Cobber*, a book about the battle of Fromelles. He argued that many missing Australian soldiers must be buried nearby. Greek-born Australian teacher, amateur historian and researcher Lambis Englezos read the book and was so touched he took up the cause, interviewing survivors of the battle and sourcing aerial photos from the Imperial War Museum that appeared to show graves behind what in July 1916 had been the German front line. The book referred to a site called Pheasant Wood or Copse just outside the village, a dozen miles west of Lille. There was a belief that a mass grave of Aussie soldiers, as well as British, was there and that a number of the burial pits had not been found after the war. He gained support for an exploration of the site from the Australian Army and the British All Party Parliamentary War Graves and Battlefield Heritage Group.

In 2007, a survey was commissioned by the Australian government. It confirmed that the pits had been undisturbed since the war and contained the remains of approximately three hundred and forty soldiers. In May and June 2008, an exploratory dig found human remains, personal effects like bibles and the remains of letters, boots, webbing, buckles, badges and buttons, and British .303 ammunition. These were in five of six pits excavated, which were then refilled. Exhumations took place from May–September, 2009, which recovered the remains of two hundred and fifty Allied soldiers, approximately one hundred and seventy-three of whom were Australian, from which DNA samples were taken.

The original site was unsuitable for reburial and a new Commonwealth War Graves Cemetery (CWGC) was built approximately a hundred and thirty yards away. At the end of January, 2010, the first body was interred at Fromelles (Pheasant Wood) Military Cemetery and the remaining bodies were buried in individual ceremonies by the Royal Regiment of Fusiliers and the Australian Army. In March of that month it was reported that seventy-five Australian soldiers killed at Fromelles had been identified from their DNA via known relatives. On July 19th, 2010, the ninety-fourth anniversary of the battle, the last soldier was buried; sadly, he couldn't be identified. The cemetery was dedicated in a ceremony attended by Prince Charles.

On 5th July, 1916, four days after 'the blackest day in the British Army's history' at the Somme, prospects of a breakthrough appeared so promising to General Douglas Haig, Commander-in-Chief of the British Expeditionary Force, that he ordered the other armies on the Western Front to prepare attacks. This was typical of Haig's dangerous optimism, which pervaded the war. On the previous day he had stated that the enemy's strength was diminishing and his reserves were worn down. To cite an example of misjudgement, ignoring the facts or just callousness, we can look at an order on the 3rd of July to attack La Boisselle at the southern end of the battlefield; this cost around one thousand men with a gain of about a hundred yards. In Haig's mind. throughout the Somme and Ypres battles, there was always the need for just 'one last push' to beat the Germans, who were always on the verge of collapse; the men who did collapse were the British and Allied soldiers struggling through the mud of Beaumont Hamel and Passchendaele .

So what had happened at Fromelles in 1916? In support of the massive Allied offensive on the Somme, the British staff had decided

German trench at Fromelles

that a strong feint attack should be made to deter the Germans from rushing troops from that region southwards to the Somme. An attack would be made from the horticultural nursery near Armentières, employing two divisions to seize the 'Sugar Loaf' salient at Fromelles. The 5th Australian Division, which had only just moved into the nursery, was therefore ordered, with the British 61st Division, to attack the 'Sugar Loaf'. C.E.W. Bean, the official Australian historian of the war, described the planning. Haking, Plumer and Munro were British generals:

Suggested first by Haking as a feint-attack; then by Plumer as part of a victorious advance; rejected by Monro in favour of attack elsewhere; put forward again by G.H.Q. as a purely artillery demonstration; ordered as a demonstration but with an infantry operation added, according to Haking's plan and through his emphatic advocacy; almost cancelled - through weather and the doubts of G.H.Q. – and finally reinstated by Haig, apparently as an urgent demonstration- such were the changes of form through which the plans of this ill-fated operation had successively passed. It was now definitely ordered. Haking arranged that the seven hours' bombardment should be begun at 11 o'clock in the morning of Wednesday, July 19th, and the infantry attack at 6 p.m. Thus the assault, originally planned to be delivered before noon, was now to be made three hours before dusk.

The lines were shelled for seven hours by two hundred thousand artillery rounds. Allied intelligence, however, had failed to pick up that the Germans had abandoned these lines and had set up new positions about two hundred yards behind them where they had built concrete bunkers that housed machine guns. The expectation was that those in the German trenches would be killed or totally demoralised from the bombardment.

The end of a bombardment was to be followed by an infantry attack, and the Germans were well aware of this. When the Allies attacked, they were hit by an artillery bombardment that left many dead in their own trenches. Those who got through had to face well dug-in machine guns that had escaped the Allied bombardment. The 61st was badly hit and its troops were forced to retire to their own lines after suffering heavy casualties. The Australians did better and reached what they thought were the German front lines, only to find them flooded and indefensible. By July 20th, they, like the 61st, had to retreat after suffering very high casualties.

The attacks were failures and, as at the Somme, very costly. In terms of manpower, five thousand five hundred and thirty-three Australians (about 90% of those involved), and one thousand five hundred and forty-seven British troops (about 50% of those involved), were casualties.

In his diary Private W. J. A. Allsop gave this account:

They lay in heaps behind the parapet or crouched under cover. Chaos and weird noises like thousands of iron foundries, deafening and dreadful, coupled with the roar of high explosives, ripped the earth out of the parapet, we crept along seeking first of all the serious cases of wounded. Backwards and forwards we travelled … with knuckles torn and bleeding due to the narrow passageways. Cold sweat, not perspiration, dripped from our faces and our breath came out only in gasps. By the time we had completed two trips, each of three miles, we were completely exhausted.

In the excellent documentary 'Finding the Lost Battalions', War Historian and Battlefield archaeologist Peter Barton featured the battlefield, and pointed out that he took three and a half minutes to get from where the Aussie and British trenches were to the Germans. And he wasn't carrying anything and wasn't under fire. He describes their task as 'impossible'. The Germans discovered on one of the captured officers an actual copy of General Haking's operations order for the attack. From it they learned that the attack was a feint, and so could immediately release troops to the Somme. The whole thing was a complete waste – especially of men. Barton also says that over one thousand four hundred bodies are still missing and that from his research into archives in Munich (of which more later) that there are at least thirty other communal graves in the area.

Whilst talking emotionally to the relative of a British officer killed in the battle, Barton also stated the problem anyone who tries to empathise with the men of the First War - perhaps all wars - have: 'I spend my life immersed in this and I have no perception of what it was like… absolutely none at all. I have an imagination, but that's faulty and it's only the men who were here who really know.'

The author can wholeheartedly concur.

Fromelles may have been forgotten in Britain but it has always been remembered in Australia together with what was going on at the same time at Mouquet Farm fifty miles or so away it was regarded as a calamity in the nation's military history and a supreme example of the British senior military bungling which killed so many Australians (and others) in the Great War. Bean commented: 'The value of the result, if any, was tragically disproportionate to the cost.'

Fromelles Cemetery
(photo courtesy of the Commonwealth War Graves Commission)

So Walter Jackson found himself at nearby Fleurbaix in the spring of 1917. An extract from the King's Own 2/5th Battalion's War Diary for March (available from the Regiment's Lancaster museum) makes interesting reading:

17th. Casualties 1 O.R.   Wounded.
18th. Casualties Killed 1 O.R.
19th. Casualties Wounded 2/Lieut. E.L.WHALLEY and 1 O.R.

As was the practice, the officer deserved a name for being wounded but the O.R. (other rank) didn't get one for being killed! It continues:

22nd. 21.40
Enemy Patrol of nine entered our trench and were immediately driven off leaving two killed (belonging to the Bawanian (sic) Regt). Our casualties Wounded. 1 O.R.

23rd. 20.30
Relieved (sic) by 4/5th Bn Loyal NORTH Lancs Regt. Our Bn going into rest billets in FLEURBAIX.

The diary then goes from the tragic to the mundane:

24th. 23
Summer time came into force (one hour advance 23 to 24 midnight).

President J.F Kennedy's favourite poem comes to mind. It was written by American Alan Seeger, uncle of songwriter and political activist Pete Seeger:

I have a rendezvous with Death
At some disputed barricade,
When Spring comes back with rustling shade
And apple-blossoms fill the air
I have a rendezvous with Death
When Spring brings back blue days and fair.

Seeger, a classmate of T.S. Eliot at Harvard and an American volunteer in the French Foreign Legion, had been killed at the Somme the previous year.

Second Lieutenant Whalley, clearly a brave man, recovered. A a typical passage from his diary shows what Walter Jackson and his pals faced on many days. The skirmish described took place on the night of June 22nd-23rd.

On the night of 22/23 a Patrol of 1 officer and 19 O.R.s, under 2/Lt WHALLEY, entered the Enemy Front Line near Fleurbaix. The Patrol proceeded along the trench in an easterly direction for about 80 yds. but finding all the C.Ts impassable and as it was becoming light the Patrol Leader decided to return, but in doing so was cut off by a hostile party outnumbering our men by about three to one. The enemy were attacked with vigor (sic) and retired. Our party returned to our lines without casualties after inflicting many casualties in the enemy's patrols.

Walter Jackson was obviously in the thick of it. He later served at Passchendaele, Lys-Scarpe, then further south again at the Drocourt-Queant Line, Canal de Nord, Cambrai and then the final advance east of Cambrai in 1918. He consistently acted with bravery, leadership and intelligence. His courage and ability were recognised and the following was published in the London Gazette in March 1920:

DISTINGUISHED CONDUCT MEDAL
240700 SERGEANT W. JACKSON
2/5TH BN. R. LAN. R.
T.F. (CARNFORTH)

He carried out many daring patrols. Under heavy shell and machine gun fire he has shown great coolness in sending back valuable information. During the whole time his unit has been in France he has trained the sniping and scouting section, and maintained a high level of efficiency.

After the War, Walter returned to his job as a builder's labourer and continued to live at Jubilee Terrace in Nether Kellet, where his wife Florence died on the 21st October, 1928, after a long illness. She is buried at Bolton-le-Sands. Walter got married again nine years later, to Blanche Tyler, who had been born in 1901 in Featherstone, West Yorkshire. They continued to live at the terrace until Walter died in his bed on 30th September, 1966. He was buried next to Florence at Bolton-le-Sands and in 1993 Blanche was laid to rest with them.

And his mother Agnes? She did not have a happy life. She moved to Blackburn, Lancashire and worked in the cotton industry, marrying George Lomas from Heywood who was in the same trade. They moved to Oldham and by 1911 Agnes had five children of her own and had adopted, in the wider sense of the word, her sister's daughter, Mary. Tragedy struck in 1913, when George was hit by a train and killed in the early hours of Thursday, 30th October. This left Agnes a widow at the age of forty-five, with children ranging in age from a baby to an eighteen-year-old.

I remember as a child and young adult the 'Old Contemptibles', the remains of the British Expeditionary Force sent to France to halt the Germans in 1914, parading with pride but decreasing numbers in the ceremonies to commemorate the war.

There are two points to be made. First, the order from the Kaiser, reputedly issued in the third week of August, 1914, to 'exterminate... the treacherous English and walk over their contemptible little army' was probably never given but was an invention of the press to anger the British and boost morale. If it was given, it would refer to the size of the British army, not its quality, and would, in fact have been pertinent. Britain's defence and international power depended – and had done for over three hundred years – on the navy. Its army, in spite of the size of the

Empire, was small and paid – i.e. professional. When the South African or Boer War broke out, first in 1880 and then nine years later, it was the first extensive land war the British had fought in well over sixty years. The earlier Crimean War was a limited one, relying on naval power, economic blockade, allies and materials superiority from our industrial revolution to achieve British objectives. In mid-1855, Prime Minister Lord Palmerston had a choice between a limited war and a 'total war' effort to destroy Russia in the field, and chose the former.

Carus House, Arkholme

George Harrison was part of this professional army. The son of Richard Harrison, butcher and cattle dealer formerly of Clapham, Yorkshire, he joined the army some time around 1898, just in time to fight in the Boer War. Richard became a reasonably wealthy man, occupying the substantial Carus House by the second decade of the twentieth century. George must have had a certain character to leave such a home for an army life. His mother had passed away by the time he was eight – perhaps even in childbirth - and this may have influenced his decision to join the army.

He was clearly comfortable with animals and became a member of the Army Service Corps, probably starting as a driver – of horses that is, not motorised vehicles. This body found its origin in the Royal Waggoners and provided transport for the army's supply of everything apart from weaponry and munitions, which were the responsibility of the Royal Ordinance Corps. George obviously did well, showing organisational as well as leadership and practical skills, and had reached the rank of Staff Quartermaster-Sergeant by the end of the decade after the Boer War. Roberts, the overall commander, wrote: 'To do justice to the excellent work done by the Army Service Corps during the war, and to give lengthy details of the magnitude of the task assigned to this department, are beyond the limits of a paragraph in a despatch.'

Another Arkholme man, Oliver Armour (an apt surname for the time and place), was part of the Army Service Corps. Dubbed 'Ally Sloper's Cavalry' by the infantry, the Corps was essential to the running of the army.

When the Germans invaded Belgium and brought Britain into the war, George was part of the British Expeditionary Force that moved to oppose them. He was then a 'Contemptible'; one of 80,000 facing an enemy at least three times as big. Somewhere alongside him was an Over Kellet man, Tom Hodgson, who survived three years of the war before succumbing in 1918. His story is in Chapter Six.

The forces met near the Belgium town of Mons on August 21st; inevitably, the British put up stern resistance, winning two Victoria Crosses on the first day and having the first fatality, John Parr from North Finchley, who was killed in an ambush alongside the Mons-

Conde canal. We will return to him. It is remarkable to note, in the light of the subsequent conflict with mass industrially produced weapons that the first German to be killed was by a sabre in a cavalry skirmish. The British were trained to hit the enemy with rifle fire of fifteen shots per minute at three hundred yards; it is reported that the Germans thought they were being opposed by machine gun nests.

The German numbers were overwhelming and on the 24th the order was given to retreat. The retreat was defended by a rearguard action at the village of Wesmes before an orderly move was made to St Vaast. Two years later an Over Kellet man, Thomas Edwards, would be a casualty of the war and be buried in what became the military cemetery at the village.

The battle of Mons has achieved legendary status in the history of the British army because of its rearguard action and its defying of the odds. A part of it that also arose was the story of the Angels (sometimes bowmen) of Mons; spectral figures that haunted the places of battle and protected the British troops. German dead were said to have arrow wounds! Despite the constant denial of the story as factual by its originator, the horror and fantasy writer Arthur Machen, it again has gone into the annals as a true depiction of a real event. Recruitment in Britain picked up remarkably after Mons.

The retreat, with the French alongside, continued remorselessly towards Paris. A successful holding battle was fought at Le Cateau, where the aforesaid Tom Hodgson was one of the defenders. The most remarkable story, however, took place at St Quentin, south east of what would two years later become the Somme battlefield. Major Tom Bridges, a cavalry officer, rode into the town and was shocked at what met his eyes. Soldiers exhausted from their incessant march were sleeping in the streets; officers had gone by train to Paris. The atmosphere was one of desperation and resignation. Bridges sought an immediate solution and came up with the idea of music. He found a toyshop and bought a drum and a penny whistle. Giving the whistle to his trumpeter, they proceeded to the town square and struck up 'The British Grenadier'. The watching soldiers, while thinking him mad, got to their feet, resumed order and restarted the retreat.

The battle of the Marne, in the first two weeks of September, halted the German advance. Sir John French, in command of the British, wanted to retreat to the Channel ports to organise an evacuation, but was overruled when Kitchener appointed the Military Governor of Paris, Joseph Gallieni, as overall commander of the B.E.F. Gallieni attacked at the River Marne, famously sending thousands of reinforcements to the area in six hundred Paris taxicabs. The French and British found a gap via the first instance of observation from aircraft between the German 1st and 2nd Armies and exploited it relentlessly. The Germans turned around and made for the River Aisne, pursued by the Allies. At the Aisne, the Germans stopped. They had a naturally strong defensive position on a south-facing ridge three miles from the river with a thick tree, scrub and bush picket in front. The French and British crossed the Aisne at different points but were stymied by the German position. Neither side could gain an advantage, nor could they retreat. Their commanders ordered them to dig in and since this prospect had not been anticipated, few had the correct tools. The immediate solution was found in local farms and the resultant trenches were haphazard holes in the ground. Trench warfare had begun.

What was called the 'Race to the Sea' was also the 'Race to the Swiss Border'; one north, one south. Each of the combatants tried to leapfrog or outflank the other but was cut off at each attempt. The result was lines of trenches that eventually stretched from Switzerland to the Channel coast. As they moved north, the opposing forces encroached on the beautiful Flemish town of Ypres. The Germans had captured Antwerp in early October, prompting the British to remove to Ypres. If the Germans could take the town and the strip from Menin to Roulers they could control the Channel ports. The struggle for the town began on October 19th and ended on November 22nd when bad weather overcame all further attempts at taking the town, with the British still in occupation.

Ypres and the area around it became the scene of continuous fighting, culminating in the Hell-on-Earth of Passchendaele in November 1917. Many lads from the Lunesdale villages were caught up in these battles, as will be described. On November 17th, 1914, one of them, George Harrison, earned a Distinguished Conduct Medal and French Military Medal for his actions outside of the town in the Ypres salient. His commendation is below.

Staff Quartermaster-Sergeant George Harrison, A.S.C., who has received the D.C.M. for conspicuous bravery while in charge of a transport on November 17th, near Ypres, is a son of Mr Richard Harrison, cattle dealer, Arkholme, Lunesdale. He served in the Boer War.

S/17867 Staff Quartermaster-
Serjeant G. Harrison, Army Serv.
Corps (Attd. Headquarters, 5th
Infantry Brigade) (LG 16 Jan.
1915).
    For gallantry and conspicuous
ability on several occasions
when in charge of the Transport,
especially on 17th November near
Ypres, under very heavy shell
fire. Has rendered good service
under all circumstances.

DCM citations database, ©Naval and Military Press Ltd 2010

CHAPTER FOUR

INEVITABLE HEROES - FRANK BOOTH

'When God made Hell he did not find it bad enough, so he made Mesopotamia; and then he added flies.' - Arabian proverb

'A hero is no braver than an ordinary man, but he is braver five minutes longer' - Ralph Waldo Emerson

Frank Booth was born in Rochdale in 1882. In 1921, at the age of thirty-eight, he had reached the rank of Lieutenant-Colonel in the King's Own Regiment, located in Lancaster. At the outbreak of war in 1914, he was based, when home, at Arkholme, where his parents George and Mary were living as tenants on the Storrs estate.

Frank's father George, or George James as he was christened, was in turn the son of James, a local chemist of Wardleworth, Rochdale. His home was a short walk from Toad Lane, where in 1844, seven years before George's birth, twenty-eight brave souls (mostly with trade or artisan occupations like shoemaker, flannel weaver or cabinet maker) formed the Rochdale Equitable Pioneers Society Limited, which soon became the Cooperative Society. The Pioneers bought basic goods such as flour, sugar and oatmeal at wholesale prices from Manchester and often wheeled them by hand the near ten miles to Toad Lane to repack and sell at minimum profit, which was then ploughed back into the business. Forty years before working men got the vote and nearly eighty years before women achieved the same, the principles of the Pioneers, such as open membership and refuting of any discrimination, were radical at the time.

It isn't clear what the Booth family thought of this neighbouring venture, but with their ongoing propensity for business and the military it seems possible that they would disapprove. Frank's grandfather James latterly became a solicitor, but his original profession as a chemist was partly passed onto George, who used the knowledge to become a leather manufacturer and tanner, in which chemicals are used extensively. This occupation seems to have taken him closer to supplies and he visited Westmorland and then settled in Arkholme a little further south. Prior to this he had made money from his invention of leather-stitched lathe belting, which replaced the more fragile cotton type previously used in machinery. George's mother-in-law was an Ormerod and that family ran businesses in the town of Rochdale; it seems that they put money into a factory George ran that produced the belts that then were adapted for the newly-invented motor bikes. By 1912, he was a Justice of the Peace and local magistrate in Arkholme.

In 1895, at the age of thirteen, Frank was sent to Rossall School on the Lancashire Fylde coast. The institution was a prime example of the Public School. Built originally for 'the sons of clergymen and others', it saw the first school cadet corps being established there in 1860, as a response to a plea from the Minister for War. It seems clear that Frank was destined to be an archetypal English cavalry officer; high church, royalist and conservative. Photographs of him taken around 1905, after he had joined the army and gone to India, show the Lieutenant with other officers in one picture and in charge of A Company of the King's Own in another. He is a striking, strong-featured man, well built, with a moustache to be proud of. His grandson, Angus Ross, has a later picture of him with his family in the garden of Storrs Hall in 1921, shortly after his return to England. He is different, obviously partly through age; but there seems to be something else. The hair is thinner, the chest less bullish; but it is the expression on his face that intrigues. There is world weariness, a coy smile and a look of resignation.

The Booths had established themselves at Storrs Hall in Arkholme in the first decade of the twentieth century as tenants at Thorneys in the grounds of the estate. Rossall School had produced innumerable officers and he became one, on the way achieving the school's Cross Flags cadet award in 1899. After Sandhurst, he joined his local regiment, the King's Own, based at nearby Lancaster, two years later and moved to India in 1903. Lieutenant Booth pursued the relatively new army requirement of signalling, qualifying in 1906 with a Special Certificate from the Army School in Poona and becoming the regiment's Signals Officer. Positions in Lebong and Lucknow followed and by 1910 he was Assistant Inspector of Signals. A year later he was seconded to the newly formed Indian Signals, and was posted to the 34th Division, Sappers and Miners. This was announced in the London Gazette on May 11th. It is interesting that at the top of the page the first announcement from the War Office referred to another character:

His Imperial and Royal Highness
FREDERICK WILLIAM VICTOR AUGUSTUS ERNEST,
Crown Prince of the German Empire and of Prussia
To be 'Colonel-in-Chief of the 11th
(Prince Albert's Own) Hussars
His subsequent military history touched a lot of people.

The years before the outbreak of war found Frank Booth at Ahmednagar, sixty miles from Poona. His wife, previously Annie York-Moore, gave birth in 1913 to a son, John Robert, who did not survive, and a daughter, Betty Edith. She was born in August 1914, a week after Germany marched into Belgium. On October 29th Turkey entered the war on the side of Germany. Frank's life was to change dramatically.

The Signallers, Frank Booth centre, second row

For centuries before World War One, Mesopotamia (now largely Iraq), had been part of the Turkish Empire of the Ottomans. Lying along its eastern border was Persia, now Iran, traditionally friendly to the British. The Arab Sheiks of nearby Kuwait and Muhammerah also supported Britain, while the Arab tribes of coastal Mesopotamia often changed sides. Germany, in the years preceding the Great War, worked devotedly at grooming Turkey as an ally, which it saw as an important part of the 'Drang nach Osten' or 'Thrust towards the East'. Germany envied Britain's empire and wanted new lands and with them fresh supplies of raw materials and markets for its finished products – a policy known as 'Lebensraum' (Living Space). The Turkish army was aided by German 'advisors', as was much of its trade and commerce.

At the beginning of November, 1914, Turkey abandoned its official neutrality towards the conflicting alliances and became a participant in the conflict, with the Sultan declaring a military jihad (holy war) against the Triple Entente of France, Russia and Britain. This was partly prompted by the seizure by the government of two ships being built for Turkey in Britain, and their replacement in October as gifts (bribes) by two German warships - *Goeben* and *Breslau*. These had then been chased through the Mediterranean by the British but had safely got into Constantinople.

The Ottoman Empire had recently been humiliated by setbacks in Libya and the Balkans. Participation in what had begun as a European war might seem to outside observers, therefore, to have been suicidal. Key elements in the government, impressed by German industrial and military power and motivated by dreams of imperial glory, greeted the expanding war as an opportunity to regain lost territories and incorporate new lands and nationalities into the Turkish Empire. War with Britain was now inevitable.

From Britain's perspective the war in Mesopotamia was originally necessary to secure oil supplies for the Royal Navy. At the outbreak of the war the Government acted quickly to protect its interests by occupying the oilfields near Basra and protecting the pipeline running from there. This occupation then, however, developed into an attempt at a less costly way – in men and money – of defeating Germany than the painful attrition of the Western Front. The result was the extension of the war not only to Mesopotamia but to the Dardanelles and Gallipoli as well.

On the 16th of October 1915, the convoy carrying the Indian

Expeditionary Force 'D' including the 6th (Poona) Division and Frank Booth, left Bombay under strict secrecy and landed at Fao three weeks later. It then moved to seize the river junction at Qurna, where the confluence of the Tigris and the Euphrates rivers is located (the Garden of Eden is said to have been between the two).

The troops, under forward divisional commander Sir Charles Townshend (or 'Alphonse' as he was known to his officers due to his love of everything French – he died in Paris in 1924), made rapid progress inland against weak Turkish resistance. In less than a month they had moved north, captured more than a thousand Turkish prisoners and lost just sixty-five of their own men. Here, contempt and complacency set in and ambition overrode caution. The Turks had about seventeen thousand men in Mesopotamia at the outset of the war and by the winter of 1915–16, the 6th British Army mustered twenty-five thousand soldiers. It had no heavy artillery and it was four to six weeks' march from Constantinople. Nixon, who was the Commander-in-Chief of the Northern Army in India and now of the Expeditionary Force in Mesopotamia, was authorised to occupy the whole province of Basra up as far as Kut-al-Amara, a town on a bend of the Tigris and at its confluence with the Shatt-al-Hai. Kut was secured in September and Nixon pressed for an advance on Baghdad itself. In passing, it might be mentioned that Nixon was another Rossall product.

General Townshend, who had become a national hero in 1895 when he was besieged in Chitral on the North-West Frontier of India, was reluctant to go on. He had reached the limit of his logistical capabilities. His medical arrangements were inadequate and the navigation of the Tigris down to Basra was impeded by low water. He was also doubtful of the quality of his Indian troops. At Ctesiphon, about twenty miles short of the capital, the Indian and British troops came up against a larger, better armed and supplied Turkish force which had had months to dig in on both sides of the river.

Townshend's force drove out the defenders, but at the cost of 40% casualties. Unable to withstand a counter-attack, let alone continue the advance, Townshend retreated back down the Tigris, with one thousand six hundred Turkish prisoners and more than four thousand five hundred wounded from both sides. The long, slow journey was nightmarish for the wounded, for Townshend had been kept short of boats and medical supplies by a stingy government in India. His over-optimistic superior, Nixon, had ordained that the men would find all they needed - but in Baghdad, which was never reached. This ragged and dispiriting retreat back to Kut-al-Amara began on the 25th of November, 1915 and they reached the town ten days later.

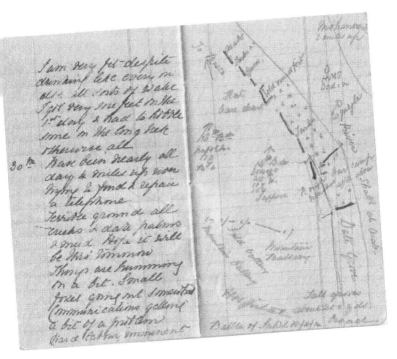

Extract from Frank Booth's diary, Mesopotamia

Private Robert Harding served in the ranks of the 1/4th Battalion Dorset regiment. He describes the march through the desert:

We are approaching the last out-post of the Basra Cantonment. The next camp is 140 miles away. Where, only the scouts know. It does not matter where; the order is to march hard and fight hard. 'Keep step, mate!' says one to another faltering in front. It is easier going in step. 'I'm dying for a drink,' says another. But the allowance is a pint a day to be drunk when ordered. We trudge on, and men bow beneath the weight of ammunition, equipment and rifle. The brazen sun burns; clothes become wet with sweat. Suddenly there is a halt. What's that? Bones? Yes, a camel's. But the others, white and glistening? A Gurkha's we are told and our plight too if we fall and faint by the way. A sergeant gives a ghastly streak and begins to charge his magazine desperately with live rounds. He is grabbed by an officer and held to the ground shrieking. 'See them? Look! Thousands of them – all charging towards us.' He struggled frantically, roaring like a mad bull until the sound makes the marrow creep. Then he falls back unconscious and the column passes on, leaving him behind until the ambulance comes.

The Turks pursued the retreating division to the town and soon surrounded and cut it off.

Captain T Clayton of the Cheshire regiment took part in the Townshend relief operations in the spring and early summer of 1916 and the later offensive against Kut. He wrote:

We learn something of the position before Kut-al-Amara… though not much, conjection and rumour filling the gap. One night was set out for an unknown destination. The day had been hot but just before just dust there came a thunderstorm and the rain was torrential. Very soon we realised that the going was unusual. On the granite like subsoil was a thick layer of mud and our feet would not stick in it. Soon men and mules were floundering in a sea of slime. Darkness closed in on a scene unparalleled, and a flickering lightening added to its weirdness. Towards the Euphrates the horizon glowed like the front of Mars. Through the long night we struggled and scrambled over the nullahs (dunes), blaspheming and cursing until the sun rose, disclosing a mob of exasperated and exhausted men, reeling through the morass towards the camp at Orah.

Captain Frank Booth, as he was now, was caught up in the siege. The town stood on a peninsula of roughly two miles long by one wide, with about six hundred and fifty randomly-built homes, shops, admin buildings and stores housing six thousand inhabitants, mostly Arab. There were no systems of rubbish disposal, sanitation or drainage. In total there were about three months' rations for the native population and army, enough to easily last until relief came; or so Townshend thought. Some were destroyed by shelling and the resultant fire in mid-December and a further quantity plus buildings on Christmas Eve.

Hunger and deprivation set in and the cold was intense. Gerald Hodgson, a local historian of Arkholme and the area around, has a copy of a painting of the outside of Storrs Hall around Christmas and New Year, some time in the first decade of the twentieth century. It shows the beginning of a foxhunt with red coats, horses, drinks, maids. Jollity and celebration. I wonder if Frank brought that to mind at the turn of 1915/16, as Kut was encircled by the Turkish XVIII Corps under their commander, the German Field Marshal von der Goltz?

British forces in Mesopotamia were now growing, the arrival of the experienced 3rd (Lahore), 7th (Meerut) and 13th (Western) Divisions bringing a significant increase in strength. These formations were ordered to advance north along the Tigris to relieve Kut. They ran into strong and stoutly defended lines and suffered some hard knocks. Although they got close to Kut on four occasions, they couldn't relieve the town. Over twenty-three thousand British and Indian troops were lost. Fighting alongside the Tigris was nearly impossible. Aubrey Herbert, involved in one attack describes the area:

'Nothing I have ever seen or dreamed of came up to the flies. They hatched out until they were almost the air… The horses were half mad. The flies were mostly tiny. They rolled up in little balls when one passed one's hand across one's sweating face… We could not speak and could hardly see.'

By February the British troops in Kut were eating the donkeys and horses, heavily disguised with curry and spices. When an officer's charger had to be dispatched, the Mess in question had the heart and tongue. The Indian soldiers had the extra problem of their religion's dietary restrictions of vegetarianism. In 1916 most men smoked and tobacco also ran out. Scurvy became a problem due to the lack of vitamin C, and Colonel Spackman, one of the doctors in Kut, reports that by this time dysentery, fever, anaemia and TB were killing twenty men a day. By the second week in April an individual's bread ration was down to five ounces, sometimes spread with anchovy sauce. On 24th of April, a last attempt to run the gauntlet by the steamer the Julnar failed; her immensely brave captain Lieutenant Commander Cowley was killed in the action.

The garrison at Kut was surrendered on 29th April, 1916. It was an enormous blow to British prestige and a morale-booster for the Turkish Army. Six days before the surrender, on 23rd April, Townshend had finally realised the extent of the disaster that was about to engulf his force. He cabled General Lake with the proposal that he should offer a huge bribe to the Turks to allow the garrison to move back to Basra, on a strict parole that none should be involved in fighting the Turks for the remainder of the war. They would instead have returned to garrison duties in India. In a muddled and panicky state of mind he cabled:

The Turks have no money to pay for my force in captivity. The force would all perish from weakness or be shot by the Arabs if they had to march to Baghdad, and the Turks have no ships to carry us there. Let the parole be given, not to fight the Turks only. During negotiations no doubt the Turks would permit of your sending up ships with food. The men will be so weak in 3 or 4 days' time that they will be incapable of all exertion, and the stenches in Kut are such that I am afraid pestilence may break out any time. Money might easily settle the question of getting us off without parole being given and it would be a great thing. The defence has been spoken to me by Khaled in the highest terms. Your decisions must reach me if you act quickly. It would take me three days to destroy the guns and ammo which I should have to do before I came away if you negotiate.

A million pounds in gold, then two million, were offered to the Turks. Both were rejected. Nothing reveals more clearly the state of mind of the General who was very largely responsible for locking up his forces in the first place, and who had little idea of the insuperable problems and huge casualties that would result. The day after surrender, two hundred and seventy-seven British and two hundred and four Indian officers, together with two and a half thousand British and nearly seven thousand Indian other ranks, were taken into captivity, together with over three thousand Indian non-combatants. Approximately three hundred and fifty badly wounded or sick men (mainly Indians) were exchanged for Turkish prisoners and sent down to Basra. It is said that Townshend's concern for the welfare of his dog Spot was considerably more in evidence than that for his troops. He even made a successful appeal to the Turkish commander that the animal should be spared the rigours of captivity and returned to Basra.

Turkish treatment of the Indian troops was originally better as the Ottomans attempted to attract fellow Muslims to their cause. During the siege, the Turks had attempted to inspire mutiny among the Indian forces in Kut by leaving bundles of propaganda pamphlets along the barbed-wire front lines calling on them to murder their British officers and join the Sultan's forces. While the British attempted to intercept these pamphlets, some did get through and led to a number of desertions. But when the garrison fell, over a thousand Indian troops and non-combatants joined the death march. In general, the Turks, Kurds and Arabs did not follow Western rules and regulations in dealing with war prisoners.

For the British and Indian troops, a nightmare began. On 6 May, 1916, the Turks and their allies began to march the British and Indian prisoners across the Syrian Desert from Kut, a distance of over a thousand miles. The historian and war poet Godfrey Elton, later Lord Elton, was a junior officer at Kut and saw the rank-and-file being marched away:

…none of them fit to march five miles… full of dysentery, beri-beri, scurvy, malaria and enteritis; they had no doctors, no medical stores and no transport; the hot weather, just beginning, would have meant much sickness and many deaths, even among troops who were fit, well-cared for and well supplied.

Mounted guards prodded over two thousand five hundred British soldiers with rifle butts and whips on the long death march. Starvation, thirst, disease, and exhaustion thinned out the British column, and only eight hundred and thirty-seven soldiers, Captain Frank Booth amongst them, survived the journey and the time in captivity. Frank's survival may have been partly attributed to the slightly better treatment given to officers; from Kut to Baghdad, for example they were taken by boat. Captain Mousley on one of the boats described an experience:

We tingled with anger and shame at seeing on the other bank a sad little column of British troops… driven by a wild crowd of Kurdish horsemen who brandished sticks and what looked like whips. The eyes of our men stared out from white faces, drawn long from a too-tardy death, and they held out their hands to our boat… We shouted out and if ever men felt like murdering their guards, we did.

Even on those officers' boats, however, the situation was often horrendous:

Every now and then we stopped to bury our dead. The awful disease enteritis, a form of cholera, attacked… A man turned green and foamed at the mouth. His eyes turned sightless and the most terrible moans came from his inner being… They died with terrible suddenness.

Of the British troops captured at Kut-al-Amara, about one thousand seven hundred and fifty died on the march or later in the camps, and of the Indian troops, about two and a half thousand. The press and subsequent memoirs described in detail the atrocities faced by Allied (especially British) POWs. Captured soldiers were herded like sheep by mounted Arab troopers, who freely used sticks and whips to keep stragglers marching. Food was very scarce, and the POWs rarely had access to fresh water. The climate of the desert where most of the campaigning took place had a debilitating impact on prisoners, especially the heat and dust. Often Turkish troops and guards relieved captives of their water bottles, boots, and uniforms, leaving the POWs in an assortment of rags – Turkish officers exercised very little control over their men. When prisoners collapsed exhausted, starved, or ill, many were left to fend for themselves in hovels. These mud-walled 'shelters' were often filled with vermin and soldiers had to resort to begging from passing Arabs for scraps of food. Many of these invalids were robbed, stripped of their last clothing and left to die.

After marching across the desert, the remaining POWs entered prison camps where they received insufficient food and faced epidemics of dysentery, cholera, and malaria. Many prisoners were simply incarcerated in regular jails with common criminals, without regard for rank or status. Prisoners sat in bare cells filled with vermin and few washing facilities. Some were marched to captivity elsewhere in Mesopotamia, others all the way to Bozanti in Turkey. Elton spoke of the Arab guards stealing the men's boots, helmets and water bottles, and of dead and dying stragglers left where they fell. Cruttwell said: 'The men were herded like animals across the desert, flogged, kicked, raped, tortured, and murdered.'

On reaching Baghdad and other towns in the Ottoman Empire, the Turks used the POWs as propaganda tools, parading the British prisoners through the streets of the capital, where their subjects could revile, stone and spit on the hated English. This public taunting of the proud British imperialists carried an important message: the British could be humbled, degraded, and enslaved. The defeat at Kut marked an important step towards the collapse of the British Empire.

One group of soldiers that continually hit bad luck and resultant suffering were the Norfolks. The 2nd Battalion of the Norfolks was at the centre of the fighting and the forced march. Fourteen hundred miles to the northwest the 1/5th Battalion had, in the previous year also suffered at the hands of the Turks. At Gallipoli in the Dardanelles they advanced rapidly but then got cut off from the rest of their comrades; it is not certain as to what happened to them in terms of death via battle or slaughter after surrender but their losses were so great that it was thought they had marched off and disappeared (see Chapter Five). In passing, the treatment of the Royal Norfolks in the Far East during the Second World War was no better. Captured at Singapore they were forced to build the infamous Burma Death railway.

The summer of 1916 saw British troops over two thousand miles apart experiencing pain, death and defeat. On the Somme, July 1st had gone down as the worst day in the history of the army. Five months later the largely volunteer troops were still being thrown against pointless targets. In Mesopotamia, part of the relatively small professional army and their Indian counterparts were, in many cases marching to their deaths in Turkey. Angus Ross, Frank Booth's grandson, tells of his mother Betty recalling her father, back at home in Emsworth, sitting for hours, sometimes days, just staring at the wall. It is not hard to imagine what he was thinking about.

In a familiar way, and responding to disaster, the British then conducted the task properly. They regrouped, rethought and planned, putting into place the entire logistic infrastructure (ships, rail, trucks etc) missing earlier. With these assets and the highly competent generalship of Stanley Maude, the British Imperial forces were able to advance and take Baghdad in March 1917, and then, eventually, Mosul.

The Turks abandoned Kut in February, 1917. As the horrors of the death marches and prison camps became known after the war, the sufferings of the men were contrasted with more favourable treatment given to their officers - Townshend, in comfortable captivity near Constantinople, was knighted in 1917. From being the hero of his country's longest siege, as facts emerged, 'Townshend of Kut' became its villain. That June, a Royal Commission reported on who was to blame for Townshend advancing so far forward. The answer was, everybody but Townshend. His commanding officer, Sir John Nixon, was censured. So too were the Viceroy of India, Lord Hardinge, the Commander-in-Chief in India, Sir Beauchamp Duff, the Secretary of State for India, Austen Chamberlain and the War Cabinet in London, which had disregarded the advice of its own Secretary of state for war, Earl Kitchener. Did Townshend have connections?

The Booth family, Storrs Hall, 1921

Now the question of how best to govern Mesopotamia floated, nay shot, to the surface. Different viewpoints were held by the military, who wanted a temporary occupation for the duration of the war, and the politicians, who wanted Mesopotamia incorporated into the British Empire. Eventually, the US President Woodrow Wilson forced the British Government along a third path it had never considered or wanted – that of carrying out a plebiscite. It was impossible to reconcile earlier contradictory British promises to the different parties involved. There were many stakeholders or those wanting influence; Winston Churchill, T E Lawrence, Gertrude Bell, Percy Cox, A T Wilson, the Hashemite Princes Feisal and

Abdullah and the Arabian Prince Bin Saud. These all tried to influence events, often in different directions, and modern Iraq and many of its problems, even the two Gulf Wars, are the result.

Frank Booth's war ended, like that of most soldiers of that era, at eleven o'clock on the eleventh day of November, 1918. Unfortunately for Frank his return to India was soon followed by a posting to another area of conflict, Waziristan. Located in what is now northwestern Pakistan and eastern Afghanistan, this rugged and remote region had fostered mountain tribes of Muslim fighters who had given the British Indian Army a difficult time for the previous sixty years. Lieutenant-Colonel Booth, as he now was, acted as the Chief Signals Officer for the largely Indian army that was sent to put down the revolt by the local Mahsud and Waziri tribesmen in 1920. There seems nothing new, if we look at the present conflict in Afghanistan or at the experience of Captain Frank Pearson's son Francis Fenwick (of Storr's Hall) in the forties. He was posted to a fort called Landikotal in the Khyber Pass and, as his daughter Sally says, '…spent the time being shot at by Afghans.' The uprising was put down largely by the innovative and effective use of airpower by the RAF. The same techniques had been used to subjugate an Arab uprising in Iraq in 1920 and 1921. I think Frank Booth would have been pleased.

Lieutenant-Colonel Booth returned to England in late 1921 and settled in Emsworth, near Portsmouth, resigning from the army in 1925. He retained a huge interest in radio communication for the rest of his life, becoming an archetypal 'ham'. Mentioned in dispatches on five occasions from March 1915 to June 1921, he served as Chief Air Warden for Emsworth during the Second War. He died peacefully in 1969.

Plaque in St Paul's Cathedral

CHAPTER FIVE

SAIL AND RETURN

'All journeys have secret destinations of which the traveller is unaware' -
Martin Buber

When Frank and Anthony Ireland, clerk and basket weaver
respectively of Arkholme, sailed down the Thames on the good ship
Otway of the Orient Line in January 1913, they must have thought
that was the last they would see of Europe, at least for a number of
years. They had caught the train from Carnforth to Lancaster and
then on to London. Thirty years later Carnforth Station would be
the focal point in the iconic film *Brief Encounter*, which summed
up the mores of the nineteen forties in Britain (it now serves
possibly the best bacon sandwich in the country). They were bound
for Brisbane, two of twelve men who would leave these shores for
a better life in what were then the dominions of Australia, New
Zealand and Canada.

Other men from the village included eight bound for New
Zealand. These were the Bibbys - Albert, Robert ('Robin') and
Frank - the Barghs - William, Charles, James and John - and George
Jennings. Stephen Parker, described in Chapter Two, and John Read
made their way to Canada. Migrants left their homelands to escape
from urban slums or rural poverty. Others sought temporary

employment to support families left behind. Some went to the Dominions in search of wealth and adventure and freedom from religious or political persecution in their countries. Their positive experiences, related in letters sent back to Britain, induced friends and families to emigrate.

The depression of the late nineteenth century had slowed down the movement of people from one country to another, but an improvement after the turn of the century had seen an about turn. The Emigrants' Information Office, opened in 1886, was the most important organization for spreading news of opportunities for life in the British Colonies and for promoting emigration, the Government giving a small grant and quarters. In turn, the colonies encouraged inward movement. Australia's immigrant population grew rapidly until the onset of World War One. Between 1905 and the outbreak of hostilities, approximately four hundred thousand new settlers arrived, principally from the traditional source of the British Isles, and the continent's population rose from four to nearly five million.

In New Zealand, refrigeration in ships opened up overseas markets for lamb and dairy products, and these and service areas needed more labour. With jobs on offer, the flow of immigrants revived. Between 1900 and 1915, New Zealand's net population gain was just over one hundred and twenty thousand, with two thirds coming from the British Isles. Bill Massey, the Prime Minister from 1912 and an immigrant from Northern Ireland himself, talked of welcoming 'the right kind of people' – those who had skills of some kind to offer.

Canada received approximately three and a half million immigrants from the turn of the century to the outbreak of World War One. In 1907, the government began to require between $25 and $50 in landing money from everyone except agricultural workers, domestic servants, and family members seeking reunification with family already in Canada. Arkholme man Stephen Parker was a gardener turned joiner who found employment with the Canadian Forestry Commission, and John Read a blacksmith who was willing to work as a farm labourer. Both fitted the bill.

In the war, there is at least some evidence that Douglas Haig, the Army Commander-in-Chief, put Dominion soldiers into situations where an objective was proving to be difficult to take. It has been shown what happened at Mouquet Farm and Pozières on the Somme when Australian troops were brought down from Messines, and at Fromelles in 1916. Also at the Somme, the South Africans were charged with the capture of Delville Wood, with horrific casualties ensuing. In November of 1916, the Newfoundlanders were given the previously insurmountable and probably pointless job of occupying Beaumont Hamel. In 1917, the Canadians were tasked to take Vimy Ridge, and they and the Australians the village, or what was left of it, of Passchendaele. Bullecourt was a disaster for the Aussies in April 1917 and 1918 saw them, with the Canadians on August 8th, trying to break through the strongest points on the Hindenburg Line.

The total number of New Zealand troops and nurses that went overseas in 1914–1918 was marginally in excess of a hundred thousand from a population of just over a million. New Zealand's first sortie in the Great War was to take Togoland and German Samoa in late August, 1914. In April of the following year, as part of the Australian and New Zealand Army Corps (ANZAC), the New Zealanders and Australians landed at what became known as Anzac Cove, Gallipoli, in the Dardanelles, which lie between the Aegean and Black Seas. This was an effort, largely prompted by Winston Churchill, to divert the war away from the increasing deadlock of the Western Front and to attack the underbelly of Europe. It was a disaster. A navigational error started the action, the Anzacs coming ashore about a mile north of the intended landing point. Instead of facing the expected beach and gentle slope they found themselves at the bottom of steep cliffs, offering the few Turkish defenders an ideal defensive position. Anzac Cove was a tiny beach and quickly became very congested. The Turks pushed back the initial ANZAC move inland. The fighting was bloody and costly. The Turks in this area were led by the unknown Colonel Mustapha Kemel, later famous as Ataturk. Lieutenant-General Birdwood, in charge of the ANZACs, asked General Sir Ian Hamilton, in overall charge, for permission to withdraw his troops. Hamilton refused.

At the same time, further south, the British and French landed unopposed on three beaches at Cape Helles, but the landing at a fourth, Sedd-el-Bahr, was a disaster. The British were caught in the fire of well-dug-in Turkish machine gunners. In addition, many British troops could not get ashore and were killed at sea. The battles over the next eight months saw high casualties on both sides due to the exposed terrain, weather and closeness of the front lines. In addition, many casualties resulted from an epidemic of dysentery, caused by poor sanitary conditions. The New Zealand Wellington Battalion reached, and briefly occupied, the high point of Chunuk Bair before being beaten back by Turkish troops, who were never again dislodged from the summit. The Allied forces eventually evacuated in December, 1915, and early January, 1916.

There are different estimates as to casualties, but certainly there were well over a hundred thousand deaths with around sixty-five thousand being Turkish and around fifty thousand British and French. Nearly twelve thousand ANZAC troops were killed or missing. Many soldiers became sick due to the conditions, suffering from enteric fever, dysentery and diarrhoea.

It was in this campaign that a commander emerged on whom Blackadder's General Melchett could have been based. Lieutenant-General Sir Aylmer Gould Hunter-Weston, KCB DSO was in command of the British 29th Division. He was noted for sending his troops into assaults that were destined to produce excessive casualties and to be fruitless. He was reputed to talk of the troops, most of whom were volunteers with no previous experience of battle as being 'blooded'; often an unfortunately apt description. Hunter-Weston was taken out of the field and returned to England after suffering with 'sunstroke'. Hamilton recorded 'He is suffering very much from his head'. He next turns up as Commander of VIII Corps at the north of the Somme, where shafts for nineteen mines had been dug from Lochnager and La Boiselle in the South to Hawthorn Ridge, between Serre and Beaumont Hamel in the north. They were due to be blown at 7.28 am, two minutes before the troops went 'over the top'. Hunter-Weston wanted the mine at Hawthorn Ridge opposite his troops to be exploded at 3.30 am. This wasn't granted but after negotiation it went off at 7.20 am, thereby alerting the German troops to the coming attack. It is now the iconic piece of World War One footage most often seen on TV; the whole ridge going up and then settling was filmed by Geoffrey Malins from a sunken lane opposite. Just before this he also filmed Lancastrian soldiers in that lane. Some of them were dead a quarter of an hour later. Hunter-Weston became an MP and died after falling from a turret of his Scottish castle in 1940.

The Dardanelles campaign also witnessed an episode later depicted in the TV drama *All the King's Men*, based on the book by Nigel McCrery. It is the story of the 1/5th Battalion of the Norfolk Regiment, which included men from the King's Sandringham estate who formed a Pals unit as a response to Kitchener's famous poster and Lord Derby's urgings. At Gallipoli in 1915, the battalion fought well and found itself in advance of other units. From that point different stories emerge from them disappearing in a cloud of dust, through a close battle at a farmhouse to them being shot or bayoneted as prisoners. As at Kut-al-Amara, as described in Chapter Four, there is definitely a feeling that the Turkish soldiers struggled with the concept of taking prisoners and then looking after them as against a policy of torture or annihilation.

When the war broke out in 1914, New Zealand had behaved as an integral part of the Empire and declared against the German aggression. Compulsory military training for males between eighteen and twenty-one had been introduced in 1909 and as a result, by October 1914, New Zealand was able to raise a force of eight thousand five hundred men to be sent as an Expeditionary Force to be placed at the disposal of the British. This body of men was sent to Egypt to await the call to fight and was combined with Australian forces to form the ANZAC, the Australian New Zealand Army Corps. In any case, men responded to the urgings of the press and politicians and flocked in their thousands to answer the call to arms and by the end of August nearly fifteen thousand had enlisted. As the war progressed and the Gallipoli venture took place, casualties increased and volunteering slowed down. The relentless deaths and injuries began to have an effect on the public view of the distant, European war and newspaper editorials urged the public to accept the need for even greater sacrifices if the war was to result in victory. Intensive campaigns to revive enlistment failed to meet their targets, with only thirty per cent of men eligible for military service volunteering.

Due to the demands of the war, conscription was introduced by the Military Services Bill of June, 1916, following the example of Britain five months earlier. Only four MPs opposed its introduction. This became an Act with effect from August 1916 and initially imposed conscription on Pakeha, a Maori word for 'of European descent' only, but this was extended to the indigenous population in June 1917. More than thirty thousand conscripts had joined the New Zealand Expeditionary Force by the end of the war. In this army there were eight men originally from Arkholme.

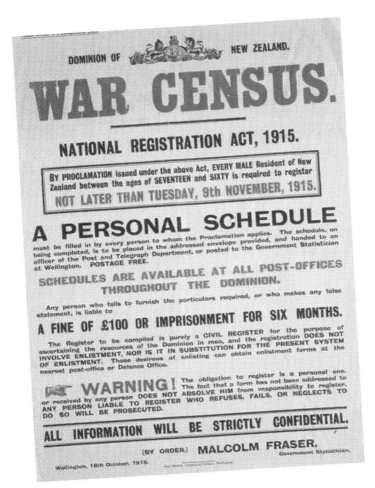

New Zealand conscription poster
(photo courtesy of the Alexander Turnbull Library, Wellington, New Zealand)

In January, February and March, 1916, it was thought necessary to form a Machine Gun Corps, as part of the Expeditionary Force on the Western Front. This was in response to the continuing trench warfare type of battle and prevailing conflict situations. The resultant Division entrained for Alexandria as a stopover on the way to France and Belgium. A central core of this Division was immediately available from the sections of the battalions and regiments that had fought in the Dardanelles. Officers and men were sent from the battalions and regiments to a machine gun school that had been established at Cairo. When these officers and men were processed through this system they were posted to the new Corps. The old Maxim guns previously used by the machine gun sections were replaced by the new Light Vickers gun.

Into these ranks came two brothers and ex-Arkholme men, Robert 'Robin', and Albert 'Bertie' Bibby. With their brother Frank, they were musical; family tradition has it that Frank was a pianist, Robert a violinist and Bertie an organist – a talent that has run down the family to reach a descendant who is a piano teacher today. Bertie also trained as an organ builder under their father Richard They all, plus mother Mary Ellen, left these shores on the steamer *Tongariro* at the start of the second decade of the twentieth century. The ship was ill fated and later ran aground, then sank at Portland Island, New Zealand, in 1916. Robert worked as a bank clerk in Palmerston North and the others settled into farming at Mangahao, Pahiatua, from where Bertie was conscripted; Robert had joined up of his own free will in September, 1915. Both were trained at Featherston in the Wellington area of New Zealand.

The third Bibby brother, Frank, was part of what was called the 37th Specialist Company. I asked Mary Slatter, who works in the Library of the New Zealand Defence Force, to shed some light on this unit, and she gave me the following information:

The Specialist Company was an advanced training group set up in the training camps to give the recruits special skills that they would need to know in order to carry out their duties, ie. signals, machine gun training etc. Since Bibby is later to be listed in his service file as being marched in from Sling Camp as in the Machine Gun Dept, it seems likely that machine gunning would have been part of his training in the Specialist Company.

So he must have pretty good at what he did.

Frank Bibby   Albert Bibby   Robert Bibby

New Zealand's first real involvement on the Western Front was near Armentières, close to the Belgian border. In September it then took part in its first major battle, at Flers-Courcelette on the Somme as part of the British XV Corps.

This was the first time ever that tanks were used and there is old footage out there of one of them rolling down the main street of the above town. As in the Spanish Civil War it is difficult to imagine savagery and killing in a place with such a pretty name – like Sevilla, or in this case Flers or Courcelette. By the time they were relieved on 4th October, the New Zealanders had advanced a quarter of a mile and captured a wide expanse of around five miles of enemy front line. Over seven thousand had become casualties, with over one thousand five hundred being killed. After this involvement, the Division returned to the Armentières area and then trained for the next major part of the conflict, the opening of the Third Battle of Ypres. It was also known as Passchendaele.

In June 1917, the New Zealand Division further distinguished itself in the storming of Messines Ridge, overlooking Ypres. After nineteen mines were blown – equating to five hundred tons of the explosive ammonal – under the ridge (the soundwaves were said to have rattled the windows of Downing Street, but this is unconfirmed) the Germans offered very little resistance. In passing, a word of warning. If you visit the area, be careful: two that were supposed to blow didn't; one later went off in a thunderstorm in 1955 but the other one is still out there.

After the explosions, the New Zealand 2nd and 3rd Brigades scrambled over the top, in and out of shell holes, and up the battered slopes. The 1st Brigade leapfrogged through, helped on the left by a solitary tank, to the final objective and took the town that gave the ridge its name. With prisoners and booty, including many guns, it was a striking success at relatively little cost, but the Germans somehow regrouped and attacked. The Division was relieved on 9th and 10th June, by which time it had lost three thousand seven hundred men, evenly distributed between the three brigades.

In the autumn of 1917, the ANZACs were given a monumental task; the taking of the village of Passchendaele. Sitting on a ridge five miles to the northeast of the old city of Ypres, Passchendaele ('Valley of the Passion' – originally Christ's, not that of the poor unfortunates who suffered and died there in World War One) was the final objective of the Third Battle of Ypres, begun in July 1917. The area had long been the place where Haig had ambitions of a breakthrough.

Here the author can express a personal interest. I undertook to research my family history a few years ago and discovered two great uncles – my grandmother's brother Benjamin Brooks and my grandfather's brother James Doohan – had both volunteered for the Loyal North Lancs regiment. They may even have been trained by Captain Frank Pearson of Arkholme, of whom more later. Ben was killed on September 20th, 1917, in a futile attack near the village of St Julien, a few miles from Passchendaele. James had been killed in a raid on enemy trenches outside Ypres on 12th January. Their bodies were never found. A lady called Annie Halliwell, of his hometown of Bolton, asked for James' possessions and was requested to give a reason why she was entitled to them. Her written response was succinct: 'Because if James Doohan had lived another fortnight, he would have been my husband.'

Albert Channing Bibby, of New Zealand via Arkholme had a strange kind of war. He was obviously doing a lot right as he was promoted to Lance Corporal in May, 1917. Unfortunately he was demoted two weeks later. In June, he was promoted again but repeated the loss of rank in August when he was two days late back from leave. He was ill all the time he was on the Western Front, suffering from what was diagnosed as 'influenza' in October and November 1916, mild dysentery in June 1917, and scabies in July 1917. In May 1918, he had pleurisy. He was declared unfit for duty and embarked for New Zealand on the *Paparoa* in August 1918. What is intriguing is that on his death in 1955, his Official History Sheet says that he died of wounds. The result of those illnesses?

So Haig envisaged his cavalry sweeping through to the English Channel coast and meeting up with an amphibious Allies unit. The area he chose had been the site of two previous battles and was largely reclaimed land and subject to flooding, and the area was not known for dry summers. A GHQ submission for a Paris conference in May, 1917, had confirmed awareness of the problems, with one sentence reading: 'Operations are liable to the danger of interruptions by bad weather.'

The New Zealand Division had been training since the end of August to overcome the numerous concrete pillboxes in this sector. A visit to the biggest cemetery on the Western Front, at Tyne Cot below the Passchendaele slope features one still in existence. It simply cannot be dismantled.

There are two spurs jutting out of the ridge, the Bellevue Spur and the Gravenstafel Spur. The latter was attacked before dawn on 4th of October and despite the mud was taken that day by the 1st and 4th Brigades. More than a thousand prisoners were taken and much equipment captured, but the attack cost more than one thousand seven hundred New Zealand casualties, including three hundred and twenty deaths. Haig, with his usual optimism (Stephen O'Shea in the wonderful *Back to The Front* describes him simply as 'a dangerously stupid man,' though the revisionist historians such as Gary Sheffield and Gordon Corrigan seem to disagree) saw the Germans as on the brink of collapse. According to Wilson and Prior in *Passchendaele the Untold Story* Haig was yet again convinced that the Germans would collapse soon. When General McDonagh, the Chief of Intelligence at the War Office, expressed doubt on this viewpoint on October the 11th, Haig launched an outburst: 'I cannot think why the War Office Intelligence Dept. gives such a wrong picture… except that Gen. McDonagh is a Roman Catholic and is (perhaps unconsciously) influenced by information… from tainted sources.' He meant Catholic; he was a Scottish Protestant. So the attack was to go ahead on the 12th.

Preparations for this attack, especially the correct positioning of the support artillery, could not be completed in time because of the mud. There was little to encourage the men as they waited overnight in a swamp with the rain falling steadily. It's not clear as to where Generals Haig, Gough or Plumer spent that night. As a result, the creeping barrage was partially misdirected, with some of the shells dropping short and causing casualties among these New Zealanders waiting to advance. When they did reach the wire it was largely uncut and covered with deadly fire, its few gaps deliberately creating gauntlets of death. Some men tried to crawl under it, some threw themselves at it, and two got right through and were killed trying to bomb the nearest pillbox. On the left there was a gain of five hundred yards of slippery slope, in the centre two hundred yards of sloping mud and on the right nearly a hundred prisoners and some blockhouses. The troops eventually fell back to positions close to their start line. For badly-wounded soldiers lying in the mud, the aftermath of the battle was a private hell; many died before they could be rescued.

Robert Bibby was in the thick of this offensive and was seriously wounded. He had already been gassed two months earlier in an enemy attack in August. The family story is that he saw a colleague about to be shot and did the ultimate by trying to shield him. To do this he must have been yards from the Germans. The bullet hit Robert and passed through him without killing him, but it hit his pal, who died. The official record for Robert describes a severe gunshot penetration wound to the chest; after field hospital he was shipped to the New Zealand Convalescent Hospital in Brighton. He was finally discharged from there in February, 1919, and sailed back to New Zealand the following month.

What is interesting is that family tradition again has it that he was shot in the stomach and nursed back to health by his sister Lucy, a qualified nurse, at Thorneys in Arkholme. The official record shows continuing bouts of enteritis, so perhaps he did have some stomach wound that produced infections from the contaminated Flanders mud.

Robert Edward Bibby was awarded the Military Cross for his actions at Passchendaele. His citation reads:

Lieut. R. E. Bibby.
For conspicuous gallantry and devotion to duty. During a critical moment in an advance he personally reconnoitred his position, leading his machine guns and men forward into action under very heavy fire, and rendered valuable assistance to the infantry.

The attack on Passchendaele remains the blackest day in New Zealand's existence. Casualties were in excess of two thousand seven hundred, of which forty-five officers and eight hundred men were either dead or lying mortally wounded between the lines. For the first time the Division had failed in a major operation. The Division subsequently continued to hold a sector of the line and the loss of life was less; before withdrawing from the front, nevertheless, four hundred more men were lost in the 4th Brigade.

The Barghs, four brothers in all, were aged between twenty and thirty-one when war broke out. William, James, Charles and John joined the New Zealand Wellington Regiment at different times during the war. They had three things in common – they were all promoted, they all showed outstanding bravery and they all got wounded. John, the eldest, who emigrated first and settled in Opunake, almost certainly took part in the assault on Messines Ridge after the mines were blown in June 1917, described in this chapter. Promoted to corporal, he was in the field at La Basse Ville a few miles from Ploegsteert ('Plugstreet' to the soldiers), north of Armentières and at the southern end of the ridge that summer. It was near here that the famous Christmas Truce took place in 1914 – if only peace could have broken out – and where Winston Churchill did his time in the trenches after his ignominy over the Dardanelles.

John suffered a gunshot wound, according to one medical report, but shrapnel in another. His youngest brother William was close by and according to the official history of the regiment was 'recommended for awards for notable acts of gallantry'. He was also a corporal by then.

The viciousness of the fighting is shown by the following extract from the same document: 'with a shout they left the trench and fell on the enemy with the bayonet. It was estimated that twenty were bayonetted: the remainder fled.'

William received the military medal in August of that year. Charles, the second oldest and a farmer near brother John in Opunake, also gained the Military Medal, this again for outstanding gallantry in the field in late spring, 1918, helping resist the offensive that nearly won the war for the Germans (see Chapter Nine). James was wounded in June 1917, and then received a gunshot wound to his right thigh in August at Grevillers, near Bapaume, on the east of the old Somme battlefield. Bapaume was an objective for the British on July 1st 1916; at least one soldier who was British born managed to get there, but over two years later.

The New Zealanders remained in Flanders until February 1918, experiencing a winter that was bleak and another failed attack, at Polderhoek in December 1917, which added to the misery. The objective was limited and defensive; capture the overlooking Polderhoek Spur which threatened the New Zealanders' trenches to the north. The enemy had numerous strong points in the ruins of Polderhoek Château and in nearby pillboxes. At noon on 3rd December, men of 1st Canterbury and 1st Otago battalions clambered out of the support trenches opposite the château, about two hundred yards away. Hopes of surprising the enemy by dispensing with the usual preliminary bombardment were quickly dashed. The men confronted, as usual, intense machine-gun fire, and although having initial success they were eventually repulsed. Casualties were high, including over seventy killed.

A further emigrant, George Jennings, was the same age as Bill Bargh, being born in Melling, next door to Arkholme, in 1894. In 1911, he was lodging at Thorneys in Arkholme with the Robinsons, whose son George married Lucy, a sister of the three Bibby brothers described above. The attractions of emigration must have been the talk of many days in the Robinson/Bibby/Jennings circle. George was working as a nursery man but emigrated in October, 1914, two months after hostilities broke out. He was keen to leave pretty quickly, giving his age as twenty-five in order to be allowed on board. George joined up in January 1916, so he was a volunteer, not a conscript – though he may have portended the inevitable. His medical report showed a defective left ear. He followed the normal route with a training stopover in Suez, time in England and then to France in September 1916. In February 1918, he was admitted to hospital with a 'perforated tympanum membrane'. This means a burst eardrum, probably from a loud noise; what that could have been on the Western Front I can't imagine. After eighteen months in Brookenhurst and Hornchurch hospitals in England he returned to New Zealand in July 1919. In November 1918, the New Zealanders marched through Belgium and in December they occupied Cologne. The war was over.

Forty-two percent of the country's men of military age served in the New Zealand Expeditionary Force. Nearly seventeen thousand were killed and over forty thousand wounded. Another thousand died within five years of the war's end, as a result of injuries sustained in the conflict.

In 1919, Field Marshal Sir Edmund Allenby said of the New Zealand soldiers (in the Sinai campaign), 'Nothing daunted these intrepid fighters: to them nothing was impossible'.

If you are ever travelling through Wiltshire look out for the carvings in the chalk – mostly of men or horses. If you get near Bulford there is one that stands out – a Kiwi. It is the friendly reminder of the New Zealanders' stay in this country and is located near their training camp of Sling. All our Arkholme to New Zealand men spent time there.

The Bulford Kiwi
(photo courtesy of the Alexander Turnbull Library, Wellington, New Zealand)

The Australian World War One experience paralleled that of New Zealand and the country's involvement has been referred to above and in Chapter Three with the stories of Gallipoli, Fromelles, the Somme and Passchendaele. It is worth looking at one more battle to show the way the Australian troops were used and their reaction to the demands. Also, one of our two émigrés was at the centre of this part of the conflict.

Bullecourt lies about a dozen miles to the north of Bapaume, close to where James Bargh would be wounded in the spring of 1918. In December 1916, French General Robert Nivelle replaced Joffre as the Commander-in-Chief of the French Army after convincing the powers that be that he could win the war 'in forty-eight hours and with only ten thousand casualties'. Lloyd George, to ensure that proper support was given to Nivelle by the British, put Haig under direct French control for the duration of the coming offensive.

At this time, as a result of a rethink by the German High Command, the German front line was moved eastwards to what was to become the highly fortified Hindenburg, or to the British, Siegfried Line and Bullecourt became a front line location. The British attacks by First and Third British Armies around Arras began on 9th April 1917, five days before Nivelle's offensive with five French armies was due to begin. Some progress was achieved, but it did not go as far and as fast as was hoped. General Gough, who had been put in charge by Haig, decided after consultation with his superior to launch another attack on 10th April in the Bullecourt Sector to put additional pressure on the German defences along the new Hindenburg Line.

The Australians, with a British-born ambulance man called Frank Ireland amongst them, and despite protestations by the Australian commanders about Gough's reliance on tanks rather than a preparatory bombardment, were ordered to attack on 10th April 1917 at 0430 hours. The main assault was to be led by the ANZAC 4th, supported by the British West Riding Division, with twelve tanks moving in advance to deal with the barbed wire and machine-guns. In a blinding snowstorm the tanks got lost advancing to the front. Such a start to the attack did little to inspire confidence, especially as Australians were in very exposed positions.

When 0500 arrived, the tanks were still not in place and the attack was postponed for twenty-four hours. Communication was poor and some of the Yorkshiremen advanced, as scheduled, toward Hendecourt. They met a hail of machine gun and artillery fire, slowly realising that the Australians had not matched their advance and subsequently withdrew, having suffered many casualties.

Gough ordered another attack for the next day. At zero hour, 0430, eleven tanks were trying to get to their positions but only three made it. The Australian infantry, supported initially by these tanks and long-range artillery barrages, broke through the German lines but then were forced to halt due to the failure of tanks to support them because of breakdown, and in one case, destruction. Further, a failure of communications allowed the Germans to surround and overcome the attackers. The Australians suffered over three thousand three hundred casualties and one thousand one hundred and seventy men were taken prisoner, the largest number captured in a single engagement during the war.

Frank and Nellie Ireland

The Australian war correspondent Charles Bean, who was assigned the role of official historian during the war, wrote: 'Bullecourt, more than any other battle, shook the confidence of Australian soldiers in the capacity of the British command; the errors, especially on April 10th and 11th, were obvious to almost anyone'.

The Second Battle of Bullecourt was fought three weeks later, the infantry of the Second Australian Division advancing east of Bullecourt village at 3.45 am on May 3rd and by the evening of the first day they had, with the Canadians in the north, made inroads into the German defences. The Germans launched numerous counter-attacks, but stubborn defence by the Australians prevented any German gain. Part of Bullecourt was seized by the British on 7th May, on the 15th, the Australians fought off a final German counter-attack and on the 17th the ruined village was taken.

One casualty was a person trying to look after others; ambulance man Frank Ireland received a gunshot wound to the head on the first day of the second battle. He himself was cleared to the dressing station and then on to hospital in Boulogne and England. The wound in his medical report was described as not having damaged the bone (skull). He was also suffering from recurring trench fever, a complaint that hospitalised his brother for five weeks in August and September of that year, 1917. This is interesting, as the illness is produced by incubating lice and is also known as 'five day fever'. That's five days for the illness and recovery. Did brother Anthony have something else?

For Frank, some good came out of it. Firstly, his wound was a 'Blighty' – serious enough to get him back to England and out of the front line conflict but not bad enough to kill him or injure him in a catastrophic way. In his case he joined the dental unit of the army. Second, he got a wife. During his convalescence he was nursed by a Nellie Prescott from Rotherham, England; they fell in love and were married in August 1918. Frank was officially discharged from the Australian army in February 1919. He and his wife went to live in Nellie's home town and he never returned to Australia.

Anthony did return on the *Beltana* in June 1919. He didn't settle, perhaps missing his brother, and returned to England. In 1924, he married Winifred Danson of Lancaster and had three children in the next eight years. He ran the Post Office from his house in Cockerham, a few miles south of Lancaster.

In 1918, now combined as a semi-autonomous Australian Corps commanded by Lieutenant General John Monash, the Australians helped to stop the German March offensive and eventually led the advance to final victory. From a population of fewer than five million, four hundred and eighteen thousand men enlisted, of which over sixty thousand were killed and a hundred and fifty-six thousand were wounded, gassed, or taken prisoner.

The Australian official historian, Charles Bean, summed up the Australian experience in the First World War by saying, 'Here Australia became a nation'.

When talking about Canadian troops, what has to be observed right away is that the Newfoundlanders were not part of the Canadian army in the First War, the Dominion of Newfoundland not becoming part of Canada until 1949. The Newfoundland Division was at Gallipoli, and then attacked at Beaumont-Hamel on the first day of the Somme battle, suffering horrendous casualties. In recognition of the unit's valour during the battle of Passchendaele in 1917, the regiment was given the title of Royal. This was the only time during the First World War that this honour was given and only the third time in the history of the British Army that it has been given during a time of war.

The Canadian's first encounter with the enemy was at Neuve Chapelle in March 1915 and in April of that year they were caught up in the Second Battle of Ypres, where the first use of gas by the Germans took place. Ten months after the Somme, in April 1917, they famously captured Vimy Ridge, which had withstood all attacks for over two years. Here, the troops got to within a short distance of the German front line by the imaginative use of tunnels and emerged in a snowstorm to take the ridge. Meticulous planning was the key, led by General Julian Byng. It still cost ten thousand casualties, but in terms of objectives achieved was a great military success. A stunning memorial sits on top of the ridge today, a tribute to the Canadians involved.

Later that year saw them taking Hill 70, near Arras and then, in November, came the last throes of Passchendaele as described above. The Canadians suffered fifteen thousand casualties fighting in dreadful circumstances after replacing the exhausted New Zealanders, winning eleven Victoria Crosses in the process. The village is peaceful today and on the two sunny July days that the author has been there it takes a vivid imagination to picture the landscape as it was in 1917. Paul Gross' eponymous 2008 film does, in its last scenes, appear to represent the terrain and carnage.

In passing, it has to be said that Passchendaele was abandoned four months later. In March 1918, cavalry and motorized machine-gun units of the Canadian Corps helped hold the line at Amiens, when the Germans launched their last big offensive. August 8th of that year saw the start of the 'Hundred Days' that began with the battle of Amiens, went through the Canal du Nord and Cambrai battles and finished where the war had started for Britain and her Dominions at Mons. Sadly, George Lawrence Price of the 28th Battalion was shot and killed there two minutes before the armistice came into place at eleven o'clock. This was just eighty-eight minutes after the last British soldier to die in the war, George Edwin Ellison of the Royal Irish Lancers; he was also killed near Mons where he had fought four years earlier at the start of the conflict. We will come back to these men.

Our two Canadian/Arkholme men had different experiences. John Read was with the 59th Battery as a gunner and fought at Vimy Ridge. He survived the war and got back to Winnipeg. Very sadly, and ironically after his experiences on the Western Front, he caught the worldwide 'Spanish' influenza and died as a result of it in January 1919. He wasn't the only one of our men who suffered this fate, as will be seen later. Worldwide, five hundred million people were affected by the virus and it has been estimated that it killed about 4% of the earth's population. It did so by producing an overreaction in the body's immune system. The stronger the system the worse the effect, killing relatively young and fit men like John Read (thirty-three years of age) more than the very young and the aged. He was buried in a soldier's plot in Brookside cemetery, Winnipeg. As he wasn't in the Canadian army at his death, he wasn't deemed to be entitled to a publicly-funded headstone.

Stephen Parker, who was born in 1877 in the cottage that was part of the Storrs Hall estate, emigrated in March 1914, sailing from Liverpool to Halifax on the *Tunisian*. He was married with a three-year-old son, Dennis James, and gave up his job as a joiner in the shipbuilding industry at Barrow-in-Furness. After only five months, in August, he was on 'protection' duties in the British Columbian Horse. Interestingly, when conscripted and attested in May, 1917, he gives his next of kin as his mother Hannah, who was still living at Storrs Cottage. He also says he was in the British Columbian Horse for six months but his dates of August to September (three months) are accepted. He then signed a waiver to his rights on account of a defective right eye. So did he 'do a runner', or did he intend to bring his wife and child over to Canada? His death information in Canada is contradictory, saying he was a widower. It also noted about him: 'Birth Date: 25 Apr 1876, Birthplace: Lancashire, England, Father's Name: James Parker, Mother's Name: Hannah Wilson, Spouse's Name: Elizabeth Margaret Clark' – so he still considered Elizabeth to be his wife fifty years after they were separated but as indicated, he was also described as a widower.

The war, as far as at least a dozen Lunesdale men were concerned, was truly a 'World' one.

CHAPTER SIX

OVER KELLET, AN UNFORTUNATELY TYPICAL VILLAGE

Or
FORM B. 104–82, and others

'I guess by now I should know enough about loss to realize that you never really stop missing someone, you just learn to live around the huge gaping hole of their absence' - Alyson Noel, Evermore

'Is it well, is it well with the child? For I know not where he is laid' - Rudyard Kipling, A Nativity

The scene was typical of countless towns and villages in Britain. It was always half expected. Class dictated how a soldier's family got the bad news of their loved one's death; an officer's next of kin got a telegram, those of other ranks the dreaded pink 'ARMY FORM B.104–82'. If the soldier was missing the form was B.104–83. Then there were the personal letters, usually from the officer who was in immediate charge on the day of death. Inevitably the soldier was a well-liked and respected individual, an efficient soldier and died very quickly, without suffering.

Naomi Leon, writing in the online Research Roots, describes how the news was received of her own great great grandfather's death:

I would have been around seven years old, an only child, and at home with my mother: father a soldier. The last year of the '14-'18 War. I so vividly remember my mother telling me to answer knocking at the front door and when doing so was handed a telegram by a telegraph boy in Post Office uniform. At that moment mother came to the door, signed for the telegram, and we both went into the kitchen. On looking back I think it was obvious that mother had guessed at the contents of the telegram as she had not opened it when the telegraph boy called.

She sat for some moments and then undid the envelope and read the telegram. How, other than putting arms around a weeping mother and joining her in her tears, can a seven-year-old bring comfort to someone who has just received a message reading, 'We regret to inform you that your husband William Finn is reported Missing, believed Killed in Action'?

The author's wife has a Korean car, a KIA. He won't be the only person in Britain who looks at the name and immediately sees the acronym for Killed In Action, KIA; sad, in a couple of ways, but true.

For two years William Finn's mother Lillie was in denial and continued to have hot water ready for her husband to bath in when he returned. Hope only disappeared in 1920 with a visit from his comrade who was with him when he died. Private James Dickinson of Duxbury, near Chorley in Lancashire, was only fifteen when he enlisted in the Accrington Pals in September 1914, against the wishes of his parents, Thomas and Margaret. He shouldn't of course have been allowed. He was killed on the first day of the Somme in the attack on Serre at the northern end of the battlefield. Tom and Margaret received Army Form B.104-83 and for years put adverts in the local paper asking for information as to his fate. His body was never found and he is commemorated on the Thiepval Memorial to the Missing of the Somme.

Army form B104-82 for John Baines, King's Own
Royal Lancaster Regiment

When Amy Beechey, of Lincoln, received the letter from Rouen just after Christmas 1917, she felt a familiar sickness and fear. The missive confirmed the worst; she had lost a fifth son, Leonard, to the catastrophe that was the First World War. She had produced eight sons and all had joined up. As well as the deaths of Bernard, Frank, Harold, Charles and Len, another, Chris, was badly wounded.

Thomas Shaw of New Cross, South East London, sent five sons to fight; the first was killed in 1914, a month after the start of the conflict. Over the next three years three more perished and the last was killed in August 1918, three months before the end of the war.

The concept of "'Pals' or 'Chums' battalions seemed a great idea when proposed by the Earl of Derby and Lord Kitchener in 1914. Mates could join up and fight together. It turned out that they usually also died together. The small town of Chorley, mentioned above, was a typical example. In 1914, it responded to the appeal for manpower by providing two hundred and fifteen men who formed C Company of the 7th (later Y Company of the 11th) Battalion of the East Lancs Regiment. The Company consisted entirely of men from Chorley and the local villages of Rufford, Croston, Duxbury, Eccleston, Euxton, Coppull, Charnock Richard, Brinscall, Withnell, Adlington, Heath Charnock, Whittle-le-Woods, Heapey and Wheelton. On 1st July, 1916, the attack on Serre proved calamitous. Of the men of Y Company who attacked, thirty-one were killed within minutes and three died within a month of their wounds. A further twenty-one (including Pte Dickinson) have no known graves and their names are transcribed on the Thiepval Memorial to the Missing on the Somme. A further fifty-nine were wounded, making a total of ninety-three casualties. The tradition of closing curtains to indicate a death was common practice in those years; it is said that the month of July in Britain saw streets with closed curtains every few houses.

Vera Brittain, the mother of the politician Shirley Williams, lost her fiancé and friends in the war. She was desperately close to her brother Edward, who delayed taking up a place at university to join in the war effort. He was badly wounded at the Somme and convalesced at the hospital in Camberwell where his sister was a nurse. He had been awarded the Military Cross. He eventually went back to the front but due to his injuries was posted to Malta. In November 1917 he was sent to the Italian Front with the 11th Sherwood Foresters after the Italians succumbed to the Austrians and Germans at Caporetto. In June of the following year, the Austrians launched a surprise attack with a significant bombardment of the British front line. Vera Brittain wrote in Testament of Youth: 'On June 16th I opened *The Observer*… and instantly saw at the head of a column the paragraph for which I had looked so long and so fearfully:

ITALIAN FRONT ABLAZE
GUN DUELS FROM MOUNTAIN TO SEA
BAD OPENING OF AN OFFENSIVE

The report went on to describe the violence of the struggle and the viciousness of the fighting. Brittain described her fear and how cold she felt in the middle of the summer day. She read between the lines of the report and realised that the attack had caught the British – including her brother – by surprise and that there would have been casualties. By the following Saturday she and her family had still heard nothing. Vera recounts the story:

I began… to think that there was perhaps, after all, no news to come. I had just announced to my father, as we sat over tea in the dining dining-room, that I really must do up Edward's papers and take them to the post office before it closed for the weekend, when there came the sudden loud clattering at the front door knocker that always meant a telegram.

For a moment I thought that my legs would not carry me, but they behaved quite normally as I got up and went to the door. I knew what was in the telegram – I had known for a week – but because the persistent hopefulness of the human heart refuses to allow intuitive certainty to persuade the reason of that which it knows, I opened and read it in a tearing anguish of suspense. It read: 'Regret to inform you Captain E.H. Brittain M.C. killed in action Italy June 15th'.

That night she looked at his picture on the wall. '…the sad, searching eyes were more than I could bear , and falling on my knees before it I began to cry 'Edward! Oh, Edward!' in dazed repetition, as though my persistent crying and calling would somehow bring him back.' (Edward Brittain was gay, and there is some evidence that this war hero was due to be court martialled when his battalion was replaced on the front. Some think he put himself in line to be killed).

John Kipling, son of Britain's best known (at the time) poet and novelist Rudyard, was killed in an attack on Chalk Pit Wood at the battle of Loos in September 1915. He was very short sighted and his father had pulled more than a few strings to get him into the Irish Guards. The battle was the last that the Commander in Chief, Sir John French, was involved in, but General Haig, as he then was, played a prominent part, even whilst plotting against French. The bombardment was insufficient and reserves were not used properly; there is dispute over whether John Kipling's body was ever found and identified. Rudyard Kipling and his wife were reputedly given the news of his death by the then Conservative Party Leader and later Prime Minister Bonar Law, and Kipling was said to uttered 'a curse like the cry of a dying man'. He was never the same again and his subsequent writings show it.

The greatest music hall entertainer of the time was Harry Lauder. There was another view on him. It was that he had a demeaning 'Highland' stage act but wanted to play the Highland Laird for real and bought extensive tracts of such land for himself and his son in Argyll. But local people cold-shouldered what they saw as a jumped-up music hall singer who had got rich ridiculing his countrymen.

His son, Captain John Currie Lauder, was a privileged child who did well and 'went up' to Cambridge. Lauder Senior used his influence to secure for John an officer's commission in the Argyll & Sutherland Highlanders, a fitting social position for a 'Laird's' son. When war came, on 4th August, 1914, John was with his father, touring Australia. A telegram recalled him to his battalion in Dunoon, Argyll. The battalion was sent on active service in April 1915 as part of the 51st Highland Division. Some say Lauder was seen as a haughty disciplinarian, a stickler for the rules and was disliked intensely by his men, though there is scattered evidence of this. On 13th November, 1916, the 51st were chosen to spearhead one of the last phases of the Battle of the Somme at the southern end of the battlefield near the Lochnager crater, blown six months earlier. The 51st attacked with such ferocity and bravery that they were henceforth respectfully known as 'The Ladies from Hell' by the Germans!

In late December, the battle finished, Lauder and his men, minus the multitude of casualties were still on the Western Front. It was cold, very cold.

The 28th of December, 1916, was a quiet day on the Somme, but it was the day John Lauder died. One story has it that he was killed shielding a private from a shell. Another version has it that he was shot from behind by one of his own men who despised him and his father as has appeared in a novel, *Empty Footsteps*, by Lorne MacIntyre.

Harry Lauder told of receiving the news:

I rushed to the door, and there was a porter, holding out a telegram, I took it and tore it open. And I knew why I had felt as I had the day before. I shall never forget what I read: 'Captain John Lauder killed in action, December 28. Official. War Office'

It had gone to Mrs Lauder at Dunoon first, and she had sent it on to me. That was all it said. I knew nothing of how my boy had died, or where, save that it was for his country.

And then, a few days later:

Realization came to me slowly. I sat and stared at that slip of paper. I had looked on my boy for the last time and this was for this moment we had all been waiting ever since we had sent John away… For a time I was quite numb. Then came a great pain and I whispered to myself over and over again the one terrible word 'dead'.

Arkholme and Nether Kellet did not experience this scenario, but Over Kellet, like so many others, did. There are different views on the effects of the war, from the 'Lost Generation' thesis to the idea of a recovery by the mid-twenties. What is true is that the impact of the death of a loved one - and usually one of a relatively young age - was devastating, as the stories above demonstrate. Picture the scene. A mother gives birth to a baby and then nurtures that child through his formative years with the trials and tribulations involved. Bullies are taken on, illnesses are nursed through and ambitions are fostered. Then the young man is put into the decision-making paradigm of either professional, well-trained, responsible military men, or, if your view is different, dunderheads who are only in the positions they occupy because of birth, privilege or connection.

The latter are then in the unenviable position of trying to win a war that has been forced on them by circumstances never seen before, in places they would not choose and by cynical politicians – or are uncaringly using the working class, to fight a nineteenth century campaign against twentieth century industrial weaponry.

Here are the simple figures. The UK lost nearly eight hundred and ninety thousand men in the war, or 2.19% of the total population. In *Death's Men* Denis Winter states the following:

As a result of the war, about 9% of males under forty-five years of age in Britain had lost their lives. The figures for the injured were enormous. One hospital specialising in the removal of steel treated 771 officers and 22,641 other ranks between April 1919 and March 1925. As late as 1928 new issues included 5,205 artificial legs for the first time, 1,106 artificial arms and 4,574 artificial eyes. In 1933 the Yorkshire Post *told its readers that 33 men had lost their sight as a result of being gassed during the previous year. Ten years after the war had ended 2,414,000 ex-soldiers were in receipt of a pension of some sort – that is 40% of all who served; and these figures were probably conservative.*

Over Kellet lost ten men in the war. The significance, again, is that the village was typical of thousands of others in Britain during these years. Men with ordinary or not-so-ordinary stories were caught up in the holocaust that was World War One and either perished or (in most cases) returned to the place they had left and tried to resume their lives. We could take any collection of streets, any hamlet, any part of a great city and it's likely that the war would be condensed in the stories and lives in those communities. We have taken three villages within a few miles of each other, two of which did in fact experience something unusual and became 'Thankful'. Over Kellet was more typical – sadly.

Newspaper reports of the dead

In 1915 local papers throughout the country began to publish obituaries of men from the area they covered. The above is from the *Lancaster Guardian*. By the following year the format was a consistent and common one, with set pages each week having columns and photographs – if available – of the deceased.

Two Over Kellet men who were killed were brothers, Thomas and Ernest Edwards, the former being the first from the village to perish in the war, in March 1916. The family history is, to say the least, an unusual one. The sons of Thomas and Agnes Edwards, they were two of nine siblings. Thomas was born in Paris and had brothers born in Scarborough, Lambeth and Ostend. A sister, Gladys, was born in New South Wales and a brother Reuben

General and Mrs Mite

entered and left the world in Over Kellet. In 1891, four of the brothers were living with relatives, the Westworths at Hall Farm in Over Kellet. Their parents were doing what they had done for many years, travelling the world as showmen with circuses. Four of the children, including Ernie and Tom, were baptised on the same day in February 1888! In 1877, Agnes had given birth to Emily who later became 'Millie the Mite', wife of 'General Mite' the Midget.

The *Manchester Courier and Lancashire Advertiser* of May 29th 1884 reports on the previous day's marriage of this couple in Manchester. According to the report Millie was born on September 1st, 1867, at Calamazo, Michigan, USA, and was thus seventeen years of age. In fact, the 1881 census shows her as living with her parents in a caravan in Grantham, being seven years of age and born in Over Kellet! At her marriage she was described as 'perfectly formed' but seven pounds in weight and less than two feet tall! Her husband, who was born in Australia or the U.S.A, depending on your source, was two inches taller, two pounds heavier, and probably two years older. A later, probably true report says that at maturity she was three feet four inches tall, weighed two stones and ten pounds and had a penchant for coffee and chocolate. Her husband, the General, liked a drop of claret, which he drank from a liqueur glass. So Millie's parents had added ten years to her age and married her off for publicity at the age of ten. After the death of General Mite in Australia in 1898, the Edwards, mother, father and Milly, continued to tour. In December, 1919, they were in Christchurch, New Zealand when Milly became ill and died of heart failure. She was buried in Bromley cemetery.

The village of Richebourg-Avoué, ten miles west of Lille, was held by British forces from the autumn of 1914, until it was overrun by German units advancing west during the great Spring Offensive in April 1918. It was recaptured by Commonwealth soldiers in September 1918, and remained in Allied hands until the end of the war. The village was less than two kilometres from the front-line trenches and was routinely shelled by German artillery. During March 1916, Thomas Edwards, brother to Mrs Mite but five feet five and three quarter inches tall, succumbed to the Germans, almost certainly hit by a shell in the vicinity of Richebourg-L'Avoué. He had, paradoxically, returned to the country of his birth, having been born in Paris whilst his parents were showing their daughter on stages and in circuses. He had been brought up in Over Kellet and had joined the army as a reservist in 1903. Called up to a Welsh regiment when war broke out, he transferred to the King's Own (Lancasters) and landed at Gallipoli with them in July 1915. He was wounded and spent four months in hospital, rejoining the 7th battalion in December 1915. He is buried in St Vaast Post Military Cemetery.

Thomas Edwards' obituary

Ernest Edwards, Thomas' younger brother, was also a private in the King's Own, being one of the recruits of the 'Kitchener Army'. His attestation papers and record in *Soldiers Who Died In The Great War* show him as having been born in Belgium. It is hardly surprising that he hid his real place of birth; Germany. He was born, like most of his siblings, while his parents were on tour. In his case it was in the town of Darmstadt in the Hesse area of the country near Frankfurt. The town later became well known for being the first in Germany to close all Jewish shops under the Nazi regime in 1933, though two of its citizens, Theodor Haubach and Wilhelm Leuschner, were executed in 1944 for their part in the Valkyrie plot to kill Hitler. Ernest Edwards died at Étaples, one of eleven thousand six hundred and fifty-eight men, in one of the numerous military hospitals at that transit and training camp. Another brother, William, 'Billy', was wounded in 1917 but survived the war.

Étaples is situated south of Boulogne on the coast, and had a rebirth in the nineteenth century from a fishing village to a rail junction. It is at the mouth of the River Canche and opposite Le Touquet, Paris-Plage, which then prospered as a holiday destination. In the Great War the area was ideal for military development and became a training and holding centre with a huge sandy field big enough for tents and a hundred thousand soldiers. It was the destination for many disembarking troops, being a day's march from Boulogne or Rouen, and developed as a medical hub, with sixteen hospitals and a convalescent unit; as a result it also fostered a cemetery. It seems it was the final jigsaw piece in the army's process of dehumanising the men and making them unthinking automatons, subject to command from above. Le Touquet became an unofficial officer's mess, except that women were allowed there; and therein lay the kernel – and often colonel – of trouble.

Wilfred Owen, the poet killed in the last week of the war, described it in a letter home to his mother:

It is a vast, dreadful encampment… a kind of paddock where the beasts were kept a few days before the shambles. There was a very strange look on all faces in that camp; an incomprehensible look which a man will never see in England nor can it be seen in any battle, only in Étaples. It was not despair or terror. It was more terrible than terror, for it was a blindfold look and without expression, like a dead rabbit's. It will never be painted and no actor will ever seize it. But it could lead to mutiny.

Recruits arrived at Étaples and were put through the brutal training regime. Very few of the instructors, nicknamed 'Canaries' because of the yellow armbands they wore, had ever been to the front, but they made up for their lack of experience with sadism and cruelty. They were, according to a soldier called Notley, 'the worst individuals you could imagine and made the men's lives hell'. They drilled the battle-hardened convalescents as hard as the new conscripts and were a hated bunch, and there was a history of conflict between them and particularly Scots, New Zealanders and Australians. The revolt began on September 9th 1917, and there are different versions of its cause and events. Some testimony has it that the spark was the arrest of a New Zealand gunner, A. J. Healy, who returned late from Le Touquet and was accused of desertion and arrested.

Vera Brittain, working as a Voluntary Nurse at one of the hospitals, wrote in *Testimony of Youth* that the nurses were told that it started when a 'half-drunk Jock' had shot a military policeman who had tried to stop him taking his girl into a prohibited café. Alan Marriott in *Mud Beneath My Boots* says that a Scottish VC winner was killed in a fracas and two military policemen ('Redcaps') were killed after being thrown over a bridge into the Canche. Crowds of squaddies gathered and more military police arrived; petrol and flames? At some stage an MP, Private H. Reeve, fired into the crowd, killing a corporal and wounding a French female civilian. News of the shooting spread quickly. By early evening hundreds of troops, mainly Scottish, and from the north east of England plus Australian and New Zealanders, were pursuing the MPs, who fled to Le Touquet. Most had seen hard fighting and death at the front.

The following morning measures were taken to prevent further outbreaks and police pickets were stationed on the bridges leading into the town. The protesters still got into Le Touquet and there were further disturbances in camp. By Wednesday the camp commander had requested help and four hundred officers of the Honourable Artillery Company (HAC) arrived, armed with wooden clubs and supported by men of the Machine Gun Corps. The strategy worked and only three hundred men broke camp and were arrested. Corporal Jesse Robart (sic) Short of the Northumberland Fusiliers was condemned to death for attempted mutiny. He was found guilty of encouraging his men to put down their weapons and attack an officer, Captain EF Wilkinson, of the West Yorkshire Regiment. He was executed by firing squad on 4 October 1917 at Boulogne and is buried in the Boulogne Eastern Cemetery. Three other soldiers received ten years' jail, thirty-three to between a week and three months' field punishments One and Two and others a withdrawal of pay and reduction in rank.

Vera Brittain again: 'Quite who was against whom I never really gathered… the village was no place for females, so for over a fortnight we were shut up within our hospitals, to meditate on the effect of three years of war upon the splendid morale of our noble troops.'

Ernie Edwards was part of the 8th Battalion that attacked at The Battle of the Scarpe, part of the assault on Arras in April 1917. He must have been wounded and taken to one of the hospitals at Etaples described above. He died there on the 16th.

The census says that Joseph Western was living at 84, Main Rd, Over Kellet in 1901, though local historian and top guy (are these villages just populated with nice people?) Bob Escolme tells me he was actually at The Row or New England cottages, the number 84 just being that number of houses the censor had processed! And Capenwray is a hamlet in the parish of Over Kellet. By 1911, he had moved to Clitheroe and was working as a house painter, but he returned to his roots and joined the King's Own at Lancaster. He died on the Somme on the 28th of July 1916, and is buried at La Neuville British Cemetery, Corbie.

Gerald Lee Booker died on the 20th of October 1916, at the northern end of the Somme battlefield near Serre. That period was one of relative calm at the Somme, being between the first use of tanks at Flers on the southern part of the battlefield on September 15th and the attack on Thiepval on the 26th. Gerald was almost certainly hit by a shell in the incessant exchange of projectiles.

He had an unusual background. Twin to his sister Viola, he was the son of John Lee Booker, an Oxford-educated barrister, and Paola Bianca Riette Malschinska, born in Georgia, the daughter of what one newspaper reported as a Polish general, though he was said to come from Tiflis, which is now known as Tblisi and is indeed the capital of Georgia. John's father, Septimus, who we will later see as a benefactor of Nether Kellet, also a lawyer, had left him the sum of £113,000 in 1884, around the £3,000,000 mark today. John eventually left over £171,000 on his death in 1942, and, as will be explained shortly, looked after his offspring financially. Paola was sued by a London milliner in 1899 and during the case in Lancaster admitted that she received £2,000 per annum from an uncle living in Paris. She was obviously profligate and had pawned some jewels which her husband had to redeem. The family spent much time in London and it was there around the turn of the century that she had an affair with a Joshua Shuttleworth. Her husband divorced her in 1902. Gerald and his elder brother Rowland lived at the family home, Swarthdale House in Over Kellet, until the outbreak of war.

Swarthdale House, Over Kellet

Gerald either rejected his father's money or was excluded from his generosity. In 1911, he took the humble path of becoming an apprentice with the London and North Western Rail Company and was given a month's trial at four shillings per week. He obviously did well and two years later was working at Crewe; his timekeeping, abilities and character were all described as good.

WIFE'S TRAGIC FEARS REALISED

Murdered by Insane Husband

The story of how a wife was murdered by her husband a few hours after she had told a doctor that she was very nervous about his mental state, was told at a St. Pancras inquest yesterday.

It was held on Rowland Lee-Booker (45), an artist, who specialised in lampshade work, and his wife Flora (40)

They lived in Bramshill Gardens, Kentish Town, where Mrs Lee-Booker was found with terrible head injuries, after Mr Lee-Booker had fallen 30 feet from a window.

The father of the dead man, Mr John Lee-Booker, of Hornsey Lane, Islington, stated that he had kept him all his life, and he was sufficiently provided for.

"He had no money sense whatever," he said. "He was subject to brain storms."

Dr. Neil Douglas Gordon, of Dartmouth Park Hill, stated that on the morning of the tragedy the couple discussed with him the advisability of Lee-Booker being admitted to a private institution because of his mental condition.

Woman's Nervousness

Mrs Lee-Booker told him that her nervousness had been increasing, because her husband was not sleeping well and was wandering around the house.

"I formed the view," said the doctor, "that he was definitely insane, but I thought he was safe to be allowed out."

It was revealed that Lee-Booker enlisted on December 31, 1914, and, as a lieutenant in the South Lancashire Regiment, served in Egypt, Mesopotamia, Palestine, and the Dardanelles. He had gunshot wounds in the right thigh, left shoulder and face.

Div. Det.-Insp. Corbett said he thought that Mrs Lee-Booker was washing an article preparatory to her husband going into a private institution, and that when she went into the middle room to get another article her husband struck her on the head with a hammer.

The jury returned a verdict that Lee-Booker murdered his wife and committed suicide while of unsound mind.

Report on the death of Rowland Lee Booker, *Western Daily Press*, August 1934

Sixteen months later he was with the Royal Fusiliers in France; less than a year after that he was dead, another life gone to the war.

Brother Rowland volunteered to join the South Lancs regiment in late 1914 and became a lieutenant in the 6th Battalion. The battalion left Avonmouth in June 1915 and landed in the Dardanelles in July. They fought at Anzac beach in August. In February 1916 they were sent to Mesopotamia, where the Anglo-Indian force, including Frank Booth (see Chapter Four) was besieged by the Turks at Kut-al-Amara. The relief force made some progress up the River Tigris, capturing Turkish defensive lines at Hanna and Falahiya, but repeated attempts to relieve Kut failed and it fell at the end of April. It is strange to think that a man from Over Kellet was fighting to rescue a man from Arkholme, thousands of miles from their homes.

A renewed British offensive astride the Tigris was launched in December, 1916, and the 6th Battalion, along with battalions of the

Loyal North Lancs and East Lancs, was heavily involved in fierce fighting to clear successive Turkish positions. The South Lancs 6th battalion was part of the force that crossed the River Diyala in March, 1917, which led to the fall of Baghdad. The three battalions subsequently took part in many successful actions and remained in Mesopotamia until the Turkish surrender. Rowland was wounded three times and the tragic results of his experiences showed themselves nearly two decades later, in August 1934. The newspaper column explains. The war had many subtle and unwanted effects.

John Alexander was brought up the son of William and Margaret at what the censor called The Square, Over Kellet, though locals would have known it as End Cottage. He travelled the short distance to the delightful village of Hornby, where the rivers Lune and Wenning form a confluence. It has a splendid castle and gets many visitors, especially in the summer months. It seems likely that John thought it a splendid place to live. He was working as a domestic servant at the Park Hotel and Inn when war broke out and he joined the Royal Garrison Artillery as a gunner. He died outside Ypres in the third battle to which that town gives its name, on the 18th of September 1917.

Hornby (left) and Ypres; sometimes, the saying 'Pictures speak louder than words' is obviously true.

For a person suffering from narcolepsy life can be difficult. No, the author didn't know what it was either, though 'sleeping sickness', its more colloquial name, could be guessed at. Tom Townson, the seventh Over Kellet victim of the Great War, was a joiner who had to cope with irregular sleep patterns. I quote from 'Narcolepsy UK':

Narcolepsy is a condition that affects approximately .05% of the population. In the UK that means 31,000 people are affected by Narcolepsy. As Narcolepsy is a relatively rare sleep disorder it is known as an 'orphan disease'. This means it a disease that affects less than 5 per 10,000 people within a community. Narcolepsy is a sleep disorder which affects the brain's ability to regulate the normal sleep-wake cycle. This can lead to symptoms such as disturbed night-time sleep and excessive sleepiness throughout the day.

Tom was known to drop off at odd moments, but people who knew left him alone and he was fine when he awoke. It could be argued that he shouldn't have been admitted to any form of military service but he was, in January, 1916, and became a stretcher bearer. He was wounded and recovered, but was hit again and taken to Le Tréport hospital towards Dieppe. The family tradition is that his sister Mary, his senior by four years, was given permission to go to France to tend to him; when she arrived in December 1917 he had already passed away. He is buried in Mont Huon cemetery with one thousand, eight hundred and forty British comrades.

Frederick William Bullough was not originally a man of Lunesdale. He was born in the small mid-Lancastrian town of Westhoughton, a place well known locally for two true historical events and one dubious one. In 1642, during the English Civil War, a battle was fought here between the troops of Lord Derby, whose ancestor called for the raising of the Pals battalions, and the

Parliamentarians. The skirmish was a precursor to the attempts to take the Parliamentarian and Protestant town of Bolton, known as the 'Geneva of the North' for its tendency towards Calvinism. The Royalists won the day and then failed twice to take Bolton. This they eventually did in 1644, and the subsequent massacre, though not necessarily backed up by numbers for the dead, went down in local history.

Derby was later captured and executed in the town's Bradshawgate; a three-legged chair he is supposed to have spent his last night on hangs on the wall of the Man and Scythe pub, a few yards from the place of execution. Visitors (including the author as an eighteen-year-old) are regaled with the threat of their demise if they sit in the said chair.

In 1812, more deaths occurred as a result of an incident in Westhoughton. The town, like many in Lancashire, had become dependent on the cottage cotton industry. Machinery was threatening this way of life throughout the country and Westhoughton was no exception. In March 1812 a group of Luddites burned Rowe and Dunscough's mill in one of the first 'Luddite' acts in Britain. A dozen people were arrested on the orders of William Hulton, the High Sheriff of Lancashire. Abraham Charlston, James Smith, Thomas Kerfoot and John Fletcher were sentenced to death for their part in the attack. The Charlston family claimed Abraham was only twelve years old, but he was not reprieved. The arsonists were publicly hanged outside Lancaster Castle in June of that year. It was reported that Abraham cried for his mother on the scaffold. The riots are commemorated by a blue plaque on the White Lion public house opposite the old mill site.

Most towns or societies have their fall guy and the butt of jokes and it's always nonsense. With the English it's the Irish, with Americans the Poles, while the French laugh at the Belgians. With

Boltonians it's Westhoughton dwellers. As a result they have a nickname for the place. The story is that a farmer from Westhoughton found one of his cows with its head stuck in a fence and found the solution by chopping its head off! Nonsense, but that's the story and that's why Boltonians refer to the place by a corruption of 'Cow's Head City'; in Lancashire dialect 'Keyedd City'!

It must have been with this somewhere in the recesses of his mind that Fred Bullough took the post of Headmaster at Over Kellet in 1913. A move to the area from the relatively industrial Westhoughton must have seemed attractive and he travelled to Over Kellet each day by motorbike from Carnforth. It then became the familiar story, replicated so many times in Britain and her Empire. A decent, 'ordinary', hardworking man responds to the call from his country, the news in the papers (propaganda?) or the blandishments or disapproval of his peers. Fred, already a drill instructor, joins up; in his case it was the 152nd Siege Battery of the Royal Garrison. Fred's profession stood him out as educated and he became an officer, in this case a Second Lieutenant. The school log for May 22nd, 1916 is in Bullough's handwriting. It reads 'School clocks put forward one hour from this morning (daylight saving)! Am leaving school this morning to join the colours at Gosport.'

His wife, Mrs A.W. Bullough, took his place and remained in situ until news of his death came to her. She resigned, but her successor was a temporary appointment until January, 1919, in the hope she would return.

In July 1917, the Battle of Pilckem Ridge, a precursor of the Third Battle of Ypres that finished up as Passchendaele, pushed the German line back, and Artillery Wood, just east of the Yser canal, was captured by the Guards Division. The 152nd, which had been in Belgium since late summer 1916, occupied this position. In October, towards the end of the battle, they were sent to a position near Boezinge close to the Yser canal and tried to move forward, but their guns became bogged down in the wet conditions and they were ordered back. On the 8th November, Frederick William Bullough was almost certainly the victim of a German shell; he is buried at what is now called the Artillery Wood cemetery.

Oak Lea - the Graham's house has the porch.
Opposite is Fred Bullough's school.

At the turn of the nineteenth century the Grahams, James and Sarah, were living at Ivy Bank in Carnforth, a few miles from Over Kellet, with their only son, Arthur James. Jim worked at the Post Office; he was obviously good at his job, as the family moved to Hayle on St Ives Bay, Cornwall, where he became the sub-postmaster. Young James worked as a messenger boy there and must have started to pick up skills in the new field of wireless (Frank Booth was doing the same in India) and showed a bent for engineering. The idea of communication, promoted by his job in the Post Office, must have kindled in James an interest in the developing field of radio.

The family moved back to Over Kellet some time after 1911

and lived at Oak Lea in the village. In June 1915, James joined the newly-formed Royal Flying Corps as a Wireless Operator. The French had pioneered the use of balloons for military observation in the early 1800s, but the British didn't follow suit until the 1870s.

On December 17th 1903, Orville Wright powered the Kitty Hawk for a hundred and twenty feet along a windswept beach in North Carolina. As with most other inventions, the human brain worked out ways of using the innovation to kill others. In Britain a young engineer named Geoffrey de Havilland was taken on to the staff at the Balloon Factory in Chatham and began to amend French planes that came in for repair. By 1911 the War Office had decided that the old Balloon Section would be expanded into an Air Battalion with its headquarters at Farnborough. Prospective pilots had to get an Aviator's Certificate which they paid for themselves (£75) before being reimbursed by the War Office! In May 1912 the Royal Flying Corps was formed and our Over Kellet man, James Graham, joined up. In 1918 it amalgamated with the Royal Naval Air Service to become the RAF.

Just before the outbreak of war, General Haig is reputed to have told an officers' meeting, 'I hope none of you is so foolish as to think that aeroplanes will be usefully employed for reconnaissance purposes in war. There is only one way for commanders to get information by reconnaissance, and that is by the cavalry'. Trench warfare, shell holes and mud proved the comment wrong and photography from planes and air-to-ground wireless communication were developed by the Royal Flying Corps so that army commanders could have fast and accurate information upon which to plan movements and artillery campaigns. On 24th September 1914, Lieutenants B.T. James and D.S. Lewis detected three well-concealed enemy gun batteries that were inflicting considerable damage on British positions at the battle of the Aisne.

This was the start of trench warfare, and in such static situations it was a huge advantage to know the enemy's positions as regards personnel and materials. It then became necessary to promote methods of concealment, and attempts to shoot down the enemy became sophisticated dog fights. The pilots became semi-celebrities and names like the German von Richthofen, the Canadians Billy Bishop and Ray Collishaw and the Brits McCudden, Ball and McElroy were household names. It wasn't advertised that many of these true heroes carried loaded revolvers to kill themselves if they were shot down in flames.

By August 1917, Arthur James Graham was a Flight Sergeant and Chief Mechanic, earning a reasonable seven shillings per week. By 1918 he had been promoted five times and offered a commission which he turned down, and had been awarded the Croix de Guerre by the King of the Belgians. He had been on leave just after the end of the war and became ill on his return; he died in a Canadian hospital in Boulogne and is buried in Terlincthun British Cemetery, Wimille, just outside the town.

The spring of 1918 saw two events happen that would cause death and destruction to swathes of people. On the Western Front the Germans launched their Spring Offensive with a type of warfare not previously seen in France or Belgium. Worldwide, people started to get a three-day fever, at the time not recognised as anything more serious. That autumn, just as the war was drawing to a close, the sickness reappeared, but in a much more virulent form. Eventually, it would kill three times more people than the war itself and would directly affect a fifth of the world's population, with no real advance in ways of curing its victims. Some of those affected died within hours of their first symptoms showing while others died after a few days, their lungs filling with fluid and they then suffocating to death. The worst affected were the twenty to forty-year-olds, which is, of course, the age of most of the military on the Western Front. In Britain, Glasgow was the first city to be affected, in May, and within weeks the 'plague' had spread south, reaching London in the next month. During the following two years, two hundred and thirty thousand people died in the country. One of them was John Edward Robinson of Over Kellet.

John Edward Robinson
(photo courtesy of the Cumbria Archive Centre, Kendal)

Grave of John Robinson,
Over Kellet

John was one of five sons and a daughter born to Thomas Robinson, who originated in Levens in Westmorland, and Hannah, from Kendal. Tom was a road repairer, and work presumably brought him gradually south, as the family was in Burton in 1901 and then Dalton in 1911, before finally moving to Cockle Hill, Over Kellet.

John served in two Corps, and the Graves Commission reports him as being in the Queen's Royal West Surrey Regiment, the precursor to the Labour Corps, though his medal record shows him as a private in the Royal Fusiliers. Either way, he then became a member of the Labour Corps and this had a huge significance. The Corps, created officially in April 1917, undertook building and maintenance of roads, railways, building structures, communication systems etc and to be in it an individual could be in less than the 'A1' condition required for the front line. That, in reality, meant that the individual had been wounded, had a disability or was too old for hand-to-hand combat. The Corps had in it every trade from carpenters and railwaymen to bricklayers, storage and transport exponents.

The author's grandfather, whose younger brother and brother-in-law were both killed outside Ypres in 1917, fulfilled the latter two criteria and served in France until 1919. The problem in being in the Labour Corps was that the personnel were usually unarmed and in exposed positions. The Germans knew just where they were, and shelled them accordingly. The Labour Corps had its parallel with Bomber Command in the Second World War; it did absolutely vital work but was deprecated and virtually ignored after the conflict, despite the fact that by the end of the war over forty thousand men were serving in it. There was an element of racism there too; many Chinese and South Africans who were predominantly black were recruited. Just under ten thousand Labour Corps men were killed in the conflict.

So that was John Robinson's experience. One of his brothers, William, also served in the war in the Border Regiment (Lonsdales). Wounded at the Somme, he recovered, returned and was injured again, and then held prisoner. After the war, in 1919, he became a policeman. His son Jack was born in 1923, and served in the Navy in World War Two.

John returned to England and succumbed to influenza and

double pneumonia nine days before the Armistice in November 1918. His father survived him by fifteen years and they are buried together with his mother in St Cuthbert's churchyard, Over Kellet.

Next to John Robinson's grave is that of a John Kitching, who died twenty years after the Armistice was signed and who, in a sense, might be another victim of the war. A woodman, gamekeeper and gardener before the war, he was another of the village's soldiers and was badly gassed. It isn't clear how much this affected his lifespan, but it certainly didn't extend it. It is hoped that he did better than John Roddy, a Manchester lad, whose father suffered the same fate. Roddy explained: 'My dad was gassed during the war and he got a pension as he could not work. One day he received a letter that said the gassing had only aggravated his chest condition, not caused it, and they stopped his pension. We got food tickets from the Public Assistance and my brothers and I all got paper rounds and the money we earned paid the rent. I left school at the age of fourteen and got a job as an errand boy in a grocer's shop.'

In the churchyard is another war memorial displaying the same ten names. Over Kellet was more a nonconformist village than Church of England, though the latter's church (as might be expected!) is more grand. Remembrance Sunday sees the village's ceremony at 12 o'clock after St Cuthbert's 11 o'clock observance.

A sad aspect of writing a book such as this is finding that a particular individual's war experience – indeed his life- cannot be determined in satisfactory detail. Such is the case with Thomas Hodgson. There were other T Hodgsons in the King's Own in the Great War, but research suggests that the Over Kellet one commemorated on the village's war memorial was born in Skerton around 1995. He survived the war from being part of the British Expeditionary Force in 1914, aged nineteen and fighting at the battle of Le Cateau, to his death in Abbeville hospital in May, 1918.

That survival was an achievement in itself. He died of wounds and is buried in the grounds of what was the hospital, a mile or so from the mouth of the Somme. It is now a bird sanctuary. Before the war he was working on his father's farm at Birkland Barrow, Over Kellet, as a cowman; amusingly, another of the people in the house in April, 1911, was a Thomas Fox, Mole Catcher!

It is a confirmation of the pandemic scale of deaths on the Western Front when two men with the same name from originally the same area are killed within weeks of each other. Thomas Corless Hodgson, whose father lived at Capernwray House, Over Kellet, suffered this fate. Like some of the Arkholme men, he had emigrated to New Zealand, in his case in 1913. I submit his obituary from the Lancaster and Morecambe Observer as testimony. In the same column a report was given of the

announcement by the vicar of the parish church that a Sergeant Escolme, a member of the church choir, was missing and was thought to be a prisoner of war.

Over Kellet and its families represented the Great War in its tragedy and pain; some ordinary lives, some less so, but all playing out the same heroic, sad and sometimes incredible story seen in so many cities, towns and villages in the country.

Thomas Corless

The cross and war memorial, Over Kellet

CHAPTER SEVEN

WHILE THE MEN WERE AWAY, BUT NOT ALL OF THEM

'No nation can rise to the height of glory unless your women are side by side with you. We are victims of evil customs. It is a crime against humanity that our women are shut up within the four walls of the houses as prisoners. There is no sanction anywhere for the deplorable condition in which our women have to live' - *Muhammad Ali Jinnah*

'The pioneers of a warless world are the youth that refuse military service' - *Albert Einstein*

As partially explained in Chapter Three, Britain's power in the world had been brought about and maintained through ships and mariners. The discoveries and settlements had created the Empire and the (Royal) Navy had maintained it in relentless and ruthless fashion, time after time. The army had been treated with suspicion by parliaments after the civil war of the mid seventeenth century, and then only sanctioned if self-financing or paid for by the monarchy. By the end of the nineteenth century it was a totally professional force, though still representing the social structures of British society, with the detrimental effects of that displayed in the

Boer wars. As described previously, when war broke out in 1914 a part – eighty thousand men – of that professional army was sent to Belgium to face the massive conscript force of Germany. Despite great valour and soldierly skill they were beaten, and had to retreat before regrouping with the French and driving the Germans back to the Aisne, where entrenchment started.

During this month, September, 1914, Lord Kitchener called for men to join up. Initially, posters were used including perhaps the most famous ever, of Lord Kitchener pointing a huge index finger at the observer from behind a stony stare.

The famous Kitchener poster

There are two points to be made. First, it was an early example of propaganda and marketing. Kitchener stares at the onlooker with an even, steady gaze. In fact, in real life his left eye wandered up and to the left as if searching for a bird. Second, its designer, Arthur Leete, produced it originally for the periodical *London Opinion*. Research by art historian James Taylor for his book *Your Country Needs You* suggested that it wasn't actually used as a poster in the usually accepted form. This is contentious, at least. In any case, recruitment was huge, peaking at 33,000 on September 3rd, just as the British Expeditionary Force (BEF) fought so hard in France. The idea of Pals or Chums battalions was raised by General Rawlinson and first tested by Lord Derby; the latter's home is actually nowhere near Derby but in Knowsley, near Prescot and Huyton in Liverpool. His call recruited four battalions of around a thousand men each to the local regiment, the King's, this taking just a few days. Unfortunately, Rawlinson witnessed, as the man in charge of the British at the Somme, the other aspect of pals fighting together; they died together too. The Accrington and Sheffield battalions attacked the reinforced village of Serre on July 1st, 1916, with catastrophic losses. The Accringtons' decimation was described as 'Two years in the making, ten minutes in the destroying,' whilst the Sheffields were disbanded before the end of the war. Percy Holmes, the brother of a Pal, recalled: 'I remember when the news came through to Accrington that the Pals had been wiped out. I don't think there was a street in Accrington and district that didn't have their blinds drawn, and the bell at Christ Church tolled all the day.' The scene was replicated throughout the country.

Recruits had to be fit for duty, five foot three or more (this had been five foot eight in 1861), and aged eighteen (nineteen to go abroad) to thirty. It's interesting to note that the typical twenty-one year old male today is four inches taller than his counterpart of 1914, who on average was five feet six inches in height. These changed as the war progressed.

Volunteers were still not sufficient to replace the savage loss of life over the next two years and by 1916 conscription had been introduced. This partially displayed an uncomfortable truth; young men were not volunteering in enough numbers for the mincing machines required for the attrition battles of the British High

Command. As Haig often said, one more push.

The Military Service Bill of January 1916 made all able-bodied men between the ages of eighteen and forty-one liable for service in the forces. By March of that year just under two hundred thousand men had been called up and conscription was in place until 1919. The effects on the social and economic fabric of the country can be imagined. Not everyone did as they were supposed to, some not reporting as directed and others claiming exemption. The Long Long Trail website gives figures for male participants in the Great War. Added up, those from the British Isles total five million five hundred and seventy thousand by the end of 1917. In 1911 the male population of Britain was just under seventeen and a half million. Expressing the former as a percentage of the 1911 population means that just under 32% of men in the country, predominantly in the economically active age range, were absent at some stage during the war years. Somebody had to replace them. Not everyone wanted to become part of the armed forces, nor was it economically wise for them to do so. Exemptions could be applied for, with each case being judged on its merits. These reports are from the Lancaster Observer in 1917:

A Farmer at Aughton applied for the exemption of his son, 19 years of age. The farm was a hundred and seventy acres with twenty milkers. He had another son, 16 years of age on the farm – Conditional exemption was granted until the first of January.

A Kellet farmer applied for the exemption of his son, twenty-three years of age and was given exemption to the 1st February.

A local electrician at controlled works was granted conditional exemption. A worker at the same works was also granted exemption. A young medical practitioner was granted exemption.

Two brothers, joint tenant farmers of seventy-four acres and who had forty-seven head of cattle applied for exemption. No hired person was employed. The Chairman asked if it would be possible for one of them to run the farm and hire a man in his place and a negative reply was given. One brother was versed in one class of work and one in another. It was suggested to the brother who appeared that he would be better employed fighting for his county and he replied that they were better employed feeding the county (laughter). The elder brother was granted absolute exemption, and the other an exemption to March 31st.

An employer who has a number of government contracts to carry out claimed exemption for a carter, but the application was refused.

Arkholme and Kellet farmers were finding things as difficult as people in the other towns and villages in the area. The Observer again:

An Arkholme farmer, 35 years of age, in partnership with his father, whose holding is 100 acres with twenty milk cows, applied for exemption. A brother (aged 14 years) was on the farm, and a second brother was called up for the end of October – Temporary exemption was granted until 1st January.

Not everyone sought an exemption on economic or social grounds; there were two other types. After conscription there were those who simply went 'missing' or failed to report to their assigned location. The others were 'conchies' or conscientious objectors. The papers latched onto the former and published lists of names – a real 'name and shame'. Perhaps those who chose not to follow the diktat given to them weren't inevitably cowards or shirkers but, in some cases the real analysts of what was happening. This is not in any way whatsoever to denigrate or cast doubt on the integrity, bravery and sense of duty of the millions who served. It must remembered that at the start of the conflict there was a huge fear, fanned by the newspapers and promoted by the government, that invasion was imminent. By 1916, that had disappeared and by late summer millions had seen Geoffrey Malins' and the unsung John McDowell's film *Battle of the Somme* reinforced the following year by the Battle of the Ancre and Advance of the Tanks. Conceived as a celebration and exhibition of victory, they became testaments to death and stalemate. Today, even revisionists and apologists for the military top brass (and political leadership?) are critical of the scale of death and injury that took place. If you were alive in late 1916 or 1917, male and aged twenty or so, and knew what was going on, what would have been your reaction? And if you were the parent of a nineteen year old?

The author has in front of him the front page of the *Lancaster Guardian* from late July 1916. Its headline, in huge type, is:

THE FOLLOWING IS A LIST OF THE NAMES OF MEN WHO HAVE FAILED TO PRESENT THEMSELVES AT LANCASTER
after being called up either under the Group System or the Military Service Act 1916.

It goes on to list nearly a full page of names with the date the individual was called up, in this case the last two days of June or first week in July. Details include ages and 'Last Address'. Name and shame again. For a reason that escapes me, although all other addresses are local, the very first one is a G. Jewitt of Parbold, Wigan. I know Parbold well; a most lovely village and understandably preferable to Albert, Messines or Kut-al-Amara in 1916. Nationally, ninety-three thousand failed to show.

The same tribunals that dealt with the above exemption applications also dealt with conscientious objectors. There were basically three types of 'conchie'. The first – often Quaker – were 'non-combatants', who were prepared to accept the call up into the army, but insisted on not having anything to do with armaments or weapons. Tribunals had power to put these men on the military register on this basis and they often were used as stretcher bearers.

Conscientious objector poster

The second were 'alternativists', who were happy to undertake alternative civilian work, but not under any military control. Tribunals had the power to exempt them from military service on condition that they actually did this work. Third were 'absolutists', those we would now term liberals, against war and conscription into the armed forces and in favour of individual freedom and civil liberty. The tribunals had the power to give these men complete and unconditional exemption. The poster sums up one view of these men, and a report from the *Lancaster Guardian* gives a different view of the hostilities:

At Bow Street Magistrates Court on Saturday, the hearing was concluded of the case in which Edward Lancestre Pratt editor of the TRADE UNIONIST and Wm Foster Watson, of the Amalgamated Society of Engineers and Ernest Hubert Williams, the printer of the paper, were summoned for attempting to cause disaffection. The prosecution was in respect of two articles which appeared in the November number of the paper, headed 'Forty Millions, Mostly Fools,' and 'Three Card Touch.' In a long speech, Watson, who denied the charge, pointed out that no action had been taken against Lord Northcliffe, Mr Bottomley and others, who, he submitted, were continually using worse phrases. The cabinet had been referred to as a lot of inept fools who ought to be turned out immediately. Pratt and Watson were each fined £25 and Williams fifteen guineas. Defendants had an uproarious reception outside court… Watson was carried off shoulder high.

It is important to note the unprecedented extent to which the state had moved in and controlled the lives of people. DORA, or the Defence of the Realm Act, gave the government a near blank cheque to run the country, via the restriction, procurement and demands for the increase in production of most things. Money was always found for the war effort, unlike for help for the poor before the conflict. The government banned kite flying, the use of binoculars, feeding the pigeons and the throwing of rice at weddings; it also limited pub opening hours, increased beer prices, and reduced the alcohol content of the same!

In 1883, T Bulmer, the Victorian cartographer, historian and compiler, produced his first directory; of East Cumberland. The directories give a sight of the place and period like opening a time capsule. In 1912 and 1913 the directory of Lancaster and district was published and makes interesting reading.

ARKHOLME-WITH-CAWOOD.

Rural District Councillor—F. Pearson, Esq.

Parish Council—F. Pearson, chairman ; James Kirkbride, John Jackson, Robt. Orr, W. Garnett, and Richd. Bownass. Clerk and Assistant Overseer, Wm. Fisher.

Post, Money Order Office, and Savings Bank ; Mark Ireland. Letters arrive *via* Kirkby Lonsdale at 7-30 a.m., *via* Carnforth at 2-50 p.m. Despatches to Carnforth 12-25 and 8-30 p.m. Telegrams to and from Arkholme Station (Midland Rly.).

Bibby Christopher & Sons, blacksmiths
Booth Geo. J., Esq., J.P., Storrs hall
Ducksbury Mr. Wm., Smithy cottage
Fisher Wm., schoolmaster and asst. overseer, School house
Gardner Miss Sarah, Poole house
Gilbody Harold, police constable
Grogan Edwd., carrier and poultry dealer, Ivy cottage
Hill Miss Sarah, grocer and confectioner
Holme Thos. Edwd., joiner, builder, &c.
Hope Miss Mary, Under Croft
Huddleston Thos., labourer, Holme house
Ireland Mrs. Margt., apartments, Lune cottage
Ireland Mark, boot, shoe, and clog maker, stationer, and postmaster
Ireland Richd. & Sons, basket, skip, and hamper makers
Ireland Thos. Mark, basket maker, Willow cottage
Jackson Mr. John, overseer, South view
Lickorich Joseph, stationmaster, Arkholme Station (Mid. Ry.)
Martin Samuel Cyrus, grocer and coal merchant
Mercer Thos. Edwd., head gardener, High Lane house
Metcalfe Richd. Staveley, vict., and farmer, Bay Horse Inn
Parker James, gamekeeper, Storrs cottage
Pearson Miss Mildred, Cawood house

Robinson Robt., contractor, Poole house
Robinson T. & Son, nurserymen and florists, Thorneys
Seward John, mason, &c., Brunthill cottage
Shepherd Rev. W., vicar, The Vicarage
Wilson Rowland, registrar of births and deaths for Arkholme subdistrict

Farmers.

Barker David, Gunnerthwaite
Barker Hodgson, Locka farm
Blacow John, Lane house
Bownass Edwd., Cort's house
Bownass Richard, Docker Park
Garnett Richd., High farm
Garnett Wm., Storr's gate
Garth Roger, Red Load farm
Harrison Richd. & Sons, Carus house
Hayton Braithwaite, Bainsbeck
Kirkbride James (yeo.), Craven view
Lawson John Duckett & Son (Geo.), Higher Broomfield
Mackereth Henry, Lower Broomfield
Marsden Wm., Gowan hall
Mason Saml. Bargh, Snab Green
Moss Wm., Brown Edge
Orr Robt. (and overseer), Providence house
Robinson Alexr., Kitchlow
Robinson John, Chapel house
Sedgwick John, Sunny bank
Thompson Robert, Cinder hill
Williamson Thos., Caulkin house

Directory page

Here are what the reader might recognise as familiar names. George Booth, J.P, is at Storrs Hall, Richard Harrison and sons (but not George) at Carus House and the Irelands are prominent. James Parker is Storrs Hall's gamekeeper, Richard Metcalfe, whose descendant's sad death started this story, is landlord of the Bay Horse and the aptly named W. Shepherd is vicar. All the councillors are men, as are the farmers, and a run through the census of the previous year would have shown all Heads of Households to be male, unless the woman of the house was a widow.

Christopher Hitchens, lately deceased journalist, polemicist and overall extremely clever person, argued constantly that the single step that needed to lift women from poverty and dependence was the ability to control pregnancy. In 1877, Annie Besant and Charles Bradlaugh decided to publish *The Fruits of Philosophy*, written by Charles Knowlton, a book that advocated birth control. Besant and Bradlaugh were charged with publishing material that was 'likely to deprave or corrupt those whose minds are open to immoral influences' and were both found guilty of publishing an 'obscene libel' and sentenced to six months in prison. At the Court of Appeal the sentence was quashed. Both the Church of England and the Catholic Church were totally opposed to any form of birth control. For those marrying as late as the 1930s and 1940s, birth control was the responsibility of men.

In 1995, Elizabeth Roberts published *A Woman's Place, An Oral History of Working Class Women 1890–1940*. The title sets the scene; an analysis of the lives of one hundred and sixty women from Lancaster, Barrow and Preston. The testimonies are of harsh existences that were repetitious and sometimes brutal – in the quip of the time – all 'work and bed'. 'The women they worked and worked,' Roberts was told, 'they had babies and worked like idiots. They died. They were old at forty.' Among the poor, wrote Ada Neild Chew, trade unionist and suffragette in Lancashire before the war, were 'women who had not lived'.

Lacking a decent education and with few employment prospects, no contraception (which usually meant years of childbearing) and few rights over property or even access to her own children if she divorced, a woman was usually left simply with one option: marriage, whether happy or not. The real culprit wasn't patriarchy but poverty. Working-class women were expected to work up until that point; then they had more children than middle or upper-class women. 'They knew their place, were secure in it, and gained much satisfaction from their achievements', which were, Roberts argues, the management of the family budget, the education and guidance of large families and the upholding of the family and local mores.

In 1914, most women's work tended to fall into traditional female categories such as what we would now call care, domestic service, nursing, teaching, sewing and secretarial work. The anomaly was the textile industry – cotton in Lancashire, and wool in Yorkshire. To these should be added the 'pit brow girls' of the coal industry. Generally, it was deemed unacceptable for married women to work.

The Suffragette movement had been growing for over a dozen years at the outbreak of war, with incidents such as Christabel Pankhurst and Annie Kenney's haranguing of Churchill in Manchester (the hall was yards from the site of the 1819 Peterloo massacre and the Pankhursts lived about a mile way). In addition, hunger strikes and Emily Davison's demise under the hooves of the King's horse at the 1913 Derby were well publicised.

Paradoxically, perhaps, in July, 1915, Christabel organised a Right to Work march. At the outbreak of war, in a visible display of patriotism, Emmeline Pankhurst instructed the Suffragettes to stop their campaign of violence and support, in every way, the government and its war effort. The work done by women in the First World War was vital for that effort.

Women played a role in a different way in the years between August, 1914, and November, 1919. The White Feather Movement harked back to the 1902 novel by A.E.W. Mason, in which Harry Faversham receives four such items and has to display acts of courage (he finds himself in the Black Hole of Calcutta at one point) to make the donators retract. It grew quickly. At the end of August an Admiral Fitzgerald gave out white feathers to thirty women with instructions to hand them out to men who had not enlisted and were, therefore, cowards. The culture in Britain during World War One was a distinctly masculine one, and any slights against a man in this way were highly insulting and aimed to shame and degrade in the same way as did the newspaper headline and list of names above.

White feather poster

Private Norman Demuth of the London Regiment, quoted in Max Arthur's *Forgotten Voices of the Great War*, had a different slant on the practice. 'Almost the last feather I received was on a bus. I was sitting near the door when I became aware of two women on the other side talking at me and I thought to myself 'Oh Lord, here we go again'. One leant forward and produced a feather and said 'Here's a gift for a brave soldier.' I took it and said 'Thank you very much, I wanted one of those.' Then I took my pipe out of my pocket and put this feather down the stem… when it was filthy I pulled it out and said 'You know, we didn't get these in the trenches' and handed it back to her. I sat back and laughed like mad.'

Attitudes slowly changed as the war progressed. Mabel Lethbridge was a munitions worker:

'When my father and brothers, uncles, relative and friends came home on leave and were staying at or visiting our house, I noticed a strange lack of ability to communicate with us, they couldn't tell us what it was really like. They would perhaps make a joke, but you would feel it would sound hollow, as there was nothing to laugh about. They were restless at home, they didn't want to stay, and they wanted to get back to the front. They always expressed a desire to finish it.'

During the war roughly two million women replaced men at their jobs. By the end, nine hundred thousand women had worked in munitions factories, a hundred and thirteen thousand on farms as part of the 'Land Army' (see below), and nearly a hundred and twenty thousand in transport, resulting in an increase in the proportion of women in total employment from 24% in July 1914, to 37% by November 1918. Location was important. Those in urban areas had more opportunities in the factories, while women in rural areas tended to be drawn to the still vital task of replacing farm labourers. Class was also a decider, with upper and middle class women more prevalent in police work, volunteer work (including nursing), and jobs which formed a bridge between employers and the lower-class workers, such as supervisors.

Food production was vital during the war years. As the land emptied of male labour, women were encouraged to step in. Women in rural areas would have been used to helping on farms around harvest time and to taking charge of milking, but they were now encouraged to operate the ploughs and do the heavy work. Of course, the three villages of Nether Kellet, Over Kellet and Arkholme were predominantly rural and agricultural in character.

Not all farmers were keen on taking on women, and the Board

of Trade found it necessary in some instances to send negotiators to persuade reluctant farm owners. They were successful; as indicated above by the end of the war the female input into agriculture was huge. Most of these women were just taken on as farm labourers, but about twenty thousand of them were members of the Land Army. Prompted by Lady Gertrude Denman, wife of the pre-war Governor of Australia, the Land Army was officially formed in 1917 to reinforce the existing encouragement by the government to take on female labour. Food production was vital, and as the land emptied of male labour, women were encouraged to step in. The Lancaster and Morecambe Observer:

Women in Agriculture:- The Board of Education have raised several objections to the Lancashire Education Committee's scheme for the employment of women in agricultural which the County Council cannot accept, and in lieu thereof, give effect to the following proposals. 1. That in future the ordinary war students receive instructions in farming, dairying, and poultry keeping, but not in horticulture. 2. That separate classes of not more than six war students be formed for the purpose of receiving instruction in horticulture for a period of one month, provided the Board of Agricultural and Fisheries will offer the committee, on behalf of the Committee for the Employment of Women in Agricultural the same grant (£3 for one month's instruction) as is made by the Board for the Instruction of women in ordinary farm work. Three that the Director of Education be authorised to grant a certificate to those students who complete the course, showing that they have worked one month at the Horticultural station at Hutton. Four, that as an experiment for three months, part time course of training in milking be arranged, provided a grant of 7s 6d. per pupil for thirty lessons be paid.

The one profession that put women near the front line was nursing. Founded in 1909, this body provided nurses for medical services in times of war. Of the seventy-five thousand Voluntary Aid Detachment nurses (VADs) at the outbreak of war, two thirds were women and girls, and by the end nearly forty thousand had seen service as assistant nurses, ambulance drivers and in catering. VAD hospitals were also opened in the cities and large towns in Britain. At first the military was unwilling to accept VADs on the front-line. However, this restriction was removed in 1915, and women volunteers over the age of twenty-three and with more than three months' experience were allowed to go to the Western Front, Mesopotamia and Gallipoli.

In 1915, Vera Brittain abandoned her studies at Oxford and enlisted as a VAD. She worked at Camberwell in London, in Malta and, as described previously, at Etaples in France. The horror of the Western Front came home to her when she was allocated to nurse a group of Germans. She also worked with a Sister who represented the old school: ''Nurse!' she would call to me in her high disdainful voice, pointing to an unfortunate patient whose wound unduly advertised itself. 'For heaven's sake get the iodoform powder and scatter it over that filthy Hun!'' The absurdity of war also hit her as she attended to a young Prussian who was to be transferred to England: 'Another badly wounded boy... held out an emaciated hand to me as he lay on a stretcher, waiting to go and murmured 'I tank (sic) you , Sister.'' After barely a second's hesitation I took the pale fingers in mine, thinking how ridiculous it was that I should be holding this man's hand in friendship when, perhaps, only a week or two earlier, Edward (her younger brother) up at Ypres had been doing his best to kill him.'

The following appeared in the Lancaster and Morecambe Observer in late summer 1916:

HOLME

Agricultural Organisation – In connection with the scheme for arranging female labour in the farming industry, a public meeting was held in the National school yesterday afternoon week, the Vicar presiding. An interesting address on the aims and objects of the movement was given by the organising secretary (Miss Rooliffe), who explained that the movement, which was non-sectarian and non-political appealed to all women who were capable of doing light work on the land. Miss E Paitson was appointed canvasser for Hole, and Miss E Peel for Farleton.

At the start of the war and during it, the Government built many new army camps. One was at Grantham, where earlier we met 'Mrs Mite' of Over Kellet and where Margaret Roberts' (later Thatcher) father had a grocery store. The camp housed nearly twenty thousand men. In November, 1914, Mary Allen and Ellen Harburn became Britain's first two official uniformed policewomen in the town, after Lincolnshire officials had requested the assistance of female police officers to protect local women from the attentions of the soldiers at the camp. When the war was over Scotland Yard tried to disband this newly-established Women's Police Service, but the moves were opposed by Miss Allen. In 1920 she became commandant of the renamed Women's Auxiliary Service with a motto of 'Set a woman to catch a woman'.

Construction was started in November 1915, on a munitions filling factory at White Lund between the three villages of Arkholme, Nether and Upper Kellet and Lancaster, and the plant opened in July 1916. It covered two hundred and fifty acres, was managed by Vickers, and was described as having 'sixteen bonded stores, a paint shop, a shellstore, magazines, a power station and six danger huts'. The function of the place was to take empty shells from another factory in Lancaster at Caton Rd and Aintree, Liverpool and put explosive into six-inch howitzers and eight-inch shells. Between them they employed around eight people and many women from the three villages worked at the factory at White Lund, including Annie Townsend, a sister to Tommy, described above.

Saul David explained the importance of the armament female labour force: 'Britain had a manpower shortage and a paucity of acetone, the key component for making cordite'. He explains that when the war became a stalemate in terms of movement, shells were needed in greater and greater numbers:

'In March 1915, at the Battle of Neuve Chapelle, the British fired more shells in a single 35-minute bombardment than they had during the whole Boer War. Britain had enough guns but it was fast running out of anything to fire, and those shells that were available often failed to explode or burst prematurely in the gun barrel. By May 1915, so serious was the shell crisis that most British guns had been reduced to firing just four shells a day and it seemed as if the war was going to be lost, not in the trenches of Flanders but the factories of Britain.'

Lloyd George, prior to becoming Prime Minister, became Minister of Munitions and set about building factories across the country. White Lund was one of them. David describes the outcome: 'By 1917, thanks to the new munitions factories and the women that worked in them, the British Empire was supplying more than 50 million shells a year. By the end of the war, the British Army alone had fired 170 million shells.' Danger and threats to health were perceived, as shown in this recurring advertisement:

Look to your Eyes!

The girl on munitions who spends hours working by artificial light, constantly peering, finds that she becomes troubled with "eye-weariness" —just a slight smarting that is usually passed by, but which, if neglected, may develop into something more serious. Interview Mr. S. Procter Leighton, who will give you helpful advice, and if needs be supply you with glasses that will relieve eye-weariness in any form. Jot down the name in case you forget.

S Leighton & Sons Ld

New Market Entrance,
LANCASTER

From the *Lancaster Guardian*

As can be expected, life in the armaments factories was tough for the women. Max Arthur quotes Mabel Lethbridge, munitions worker, again:

I was put into a shell-filling shed where I was taught to fill 18-pounder shells. We girls never went into a shed unless there were some of the older workers there to help us, but the older workers were always moaning. They were upset and miserable because there had been so many explosions, and I think they were justified, as we heard that machines we were going to be asked to work had been condemned.

We were continually searched for cigarettes, matches and anything you might have as metal... There was a great feeling of tension all the time, although it was not exactly fear as we were very merry and always singing and very gay. The only difficulty I found was when I was put on one of these machines was that it was very tiring work. The shells were very heavy, and we had to kneel down in front of the machine. When you stood up you just felt you hadn't got any knees, and you hadn't got any back, except one aching mass. That was from all the carrying, the long hours and the weight.

On October 1st 1917, White Lund exploded. Wartime censorship meant that further details were not forthcoming, and only after the war did more of the facts emerge. The cause of the fire which triggered the explosions was not discovered, but it was thought that it might have been a match carelessly thrown away after lighting a cigarette – this despite stringent security checks on staff entering the White Lund factory, just as described by Mabel Lethbridge above. There were acts of heroism. There were ten deaths, mainly of firemen, with two seriously injured, and the Lancaster and Morecambe Fire Brigades subsequently received nine OBEs; a BEM was awarded to a female telephonist who remained on duty for throughout the crisis. Other heroes emerged; Abraham Clarke Graham and Thomas Kew were off-duty railwaymen and heard the alarm; seeing a fully-loaded train close to the fire zone, they were well aware of the risk of further explosions. They removed fifty-four wagons from the danger zone, despite some of them being ablaze and exploding, and some needing uncoupling before moving. The two men worked relentlessly for about three hours and no doubt averted an even greater disaster. They received the Edward Medal from King George V in May, 1918. The two were great examples of exemptions to conscription.

The strength of the blast can only be guessed at. The tremor was felt at Burnley, twenty-five miles away, and fires could be seen as far away as Barrow in Furness. The last explosion was at 4 am on the 3rd of October. In Lancaster, police went from door to door ordering people to evacuate to Lancaster Moor, while others fled to the countryside as shells hissed overhead and neighbouring villages were inundated with tired and cold evacuees.

It was the same story in Morecambe, with people congregating on the promenade, many half-dressed. Bob Escolme tells of playing in shell holes in later years, in Torrisholme, Morecambe, where projectiles had landed. Apparently the craters made excellent tobogganing sites!

Bob goes on:

"Kellet is fortunate to have its own eyewitness account. Edith Lewis was an intelligent teenager in 1917, and her memory was unimpaired when I got this account from her in 2002. Her memory and other faculties were seemingly unimpaired until very near her death aged 108. This is the account she gave me:

'Mrs Hobson of Tomlinson Row was more distressed than most. She fled the reservoir at Pedder Pots taking her bank book with her, presumably to throw herself into the water, (as) if the world was coming to an end. The school log reports October 2, School closed all day (only 12 children came), all of whom had been deprived of their sleep the previous night... As the explosions had not ceased and there was still danger ahead, it was thought advisable to close school for the day. Because of the wartime censorship, the local press was only allowed to print a brief statement that a serious fire and an explosion had occurred at a munition factory in the North of England.'

"Mrs Lewis's recollections of the panic that the explosions caused are borne out by the press reports that appeared much later. Eye witnesses in Morecambe and Lancaster confirmed what Edith remembers. Morecambe promenade and foreshore was crowded with scantily clad and frightened people; likewise the moor at Lancaster. Fifteen people died in the explosions and fires. Shells hissed overhead, the ground shook form the explosions and these were felt as far afield as Burnley and the fires were seen at Barrow. The cause of the explosion was never satisfactorily explained."

Villagers played their part in the war effort in other ways. Bob Escolme again: 'There were thirty men from the parish, 18 or over who served. At a rough estimate this was half the male population. I do not have many names of parishioners who served the war effort as civilians. Cecil Taylor (a sweet pea grower before the war) worked at the munition factory in Lancaster. Cecil's future wife Sarah Thexton worked at Waring and Gillow's, the renowned furniture makers. She stitched linen fabric onto wooden struts for planes, and her sister 'doped' the fabric. With many domestics finding more remunerative work in the factories, combined with the male service recruitment (there was a shortage of manpower). An illustration: the church clerk and sexton was Thomas Howarth. He had held both positions for 30 years. He gave word to the vicar, M.S. Bell, in 1917 that he could no longer dig graves. No one else was prepared to do it. Bell took legal advice: relatives would have to prepare the deceased's grave themselves.'

Children did their bit. At school they knitted socks, balaclavas and gloves for the troops. The parish magazine came in some bizarre colours late in the war as a paper shortage saw unsuitable paper for normal use being printed on.

The vicar of Over Kellet from 1917 was an ex-army chaplain invalided out (health, not a war injury). His newsletter gave a low-key response to the Armistice, quoting in full Tennyson's 'Ring Out Wild Bells'. He added: 'The children received the news of the end of the war with 'enthusiasm' and cheered the Union Jack. They were allowed to climb the church tower, and watched the efforts of the amateur campanologists with interest. Celebrations in a war-weary Kellet were muted.'

Advertisements from the *Lancaster Guardian*, 1917

The attitude to women doing 'men's' work was somewhat patronising (or was it paternal?) as a series of advertisements for a wholesome drink show.

Subsequent adverts featured women in different roles that were available to them due to the shortage of men. In the local newspapers, the 'positions vacant' columns had changed in character. They required men 'above the age for military service' or women with 'no children and a husband abroad'. Sometimes the jobs were advertised as 'for the duration' and one can see the attempt at loyalty in that. Farming would consider females 'who were used to hard work'.

Another company had a traditional take on domestic life with a nice twist towards recognising the labour shortage! In 1916, the *Liverpool Echo* published an article about women's changing attitudes as a result of the war with a different slant – the increase in drinking. Entitled 'Light On The Ways Of Women Drinkers', it drew attention to the growing trend for females to call in at the pub, often after work, and recommended courses of action to overcome it, including the 'fitting of clear windows and the removal of partitions, snugs and other obstacles likely to facilitate secret drinking.'

After the war, women were expected to give way to men returning from the forces and return to pre-war 'women's work', and the assumption came back that a woman's place was in the home. The percentage of women at work returned closely to pre-war levels, but more women than before worked in offices. World War One hastened the collapse of one type of traditional women's employment and with it pushed a change of attitudes towards females. This was domestic service. From the nineteenth century to 1911, between 11% and 13% of the female population in England and Wales were domestic servants. By 1931, the percentage had dropped to under eight.

After the war, shorter skirts and hair became fashionable (bear in mind there is a historical argument that the length of women's skirts has a direct correlation with economic performance. The sixties saw a booming economy and the female thigh; perhaps there's some truth in it!) Women over thirty years of age, despite the fact that the wartime 'male substitute workers' were predominantly under this marker, could vote, and went out with men without a chaperone and as well as smoking, as described, wore make-up in public for the first time. In 1919, being female or married was no longer allowed to disqualify someone from holding a job in the professions or civil service, the Sex Disqualification (Removal) Act of 1919 dictating this, but this was offset to some extent by the 1919 Restoration of Pre-War Practices Act. This forced most women to leave their wartime roles as men came home and factories switched to peacetime production. Women were finally awarded degrees at Oxford in 1920 (at the same time females at Cambridge were refused again, having to settle for titles of degrees only, called, predictably, the 'BA Tit').

By 1931, female wage rates were back to their pre-war levels of half those of men in most occupations.

In the villages of Nether Kellet, Over Kellet and Arkholme, just as in the rest of the country, the French phrase 'plus ça change, plus c'est la même chose' (the greater the change, the more things remain the same) seems to have applied to women and society. It can also mean 'history repeats itself'. In a wider sense it did, in 1939.

CHAPTER EIGHT

THEY ALSO SERVED
AND RETURNED

'It's a thing to see when a boy comes home' -
John Steinbeck, The Grapes of Wrath

In writing a book such as this, the author is at pains to try to elevate the people involved (in this case a total of ninety on two plaques and a memorial) to the status of humans with real flesh and blood, emotions and feelings and the pains and happiness of living a life. Those lives, at that time, had uniqueness in their historical context and I have striven to do justice to their experiences.

Thus it was with the death of Bertie Hainsworth, ten years after the war ended. Bertie was the son of Elizabeth, née Clough, and was presumably bright and well educated. Why this assumption? Because his mother was a schoolmistress, who in 1881 was teaching near her place of birth in Methley, West Yorkshire.

From here on, some guesswork is involved. She married and became Mrs Hainsworth and eventually had at least three children, Bertie being the youngest. By 1891, she was in Arkholme, living at the National Schoolhouse in Chapel Lane with her mother Eliza and brother Edward Clough, who was the schoolmaster. With her were Marie and Doris, who was born in 1890; but there was no father around. Ten years later 'Maria', as the census has her, is still there and Bertie is now around, born in Kendal in 1892. The year 1911 sees mum, Doris and Bertie in Lancaster with Bertie an apprentice coach builder. Elizabeth is a retired schoolmistress and a widow. Conclusion? There is further guesswork suggesting that the father of the Hainsworth's is away a lot and is a soldier or sailor. I will plump for the latter, because that is what Bertie became. In the Great War he joined the navy and survived it, which actually wasn't as difficult as doing the same in the army.

So after the war Bertie joined the Merchant Navy. He qualified in the new art of radio, as did our other men, Frank Booth of Arkholme and James Graham of Over Kellet. At some stage he lived in Cardiff - and then came the accident. At the end of 1928 he was on the ship the *Konsanti* on the River Parana off the coast of Argentina. Despite his experience, he fell overboard and perished; the comment on his death says 'drowning due to drink'. I wondered how this could be. Was he depressed? Homesick? Then, in small writing, I saw the date; 31/12/1928. He'd probably been bringing in the New Year. Sad.

As partially shown in Chapters Three and Seven, Britain had depended for centuries on the Senior Service, the Navy, for its pre-eminent world position. It was this that enabled it to maintain its empire with a relatively small army. In *How One Small Country Built the Modern World*, Harry Bingham explains this predominance. As an introduction he cites the example of a confrontation in February 1758 between a ninety-year-old, sixty-four gun ship of the line, the Monmouth, and the brand new, eighty-gun, state-of-the-art French ship the *Foudroyant*, off south-eastern Spain. After four hours of fighting, the *Monmouth*, with final help from a sister ship, battered its opponent into submission. How? The difference was the rate of fire of the two ships. Why the difference?

First, the training, experience, discipline, leadership and ethos. All the complex interlocking parts of manning, leadership, infrastructure, finance and the rest were as well engineered as it was possible to be.' Second, it was down to 'the nature and purpose of the (two) rival navies. For the French,' (read other countries) 'the navy was a means to an end. It was there to convey troops, support troops, allow troops to land… For the British the purpose of the Royal Navy was simply this: to prevent invasion. Given that overriding central purpose, then gunnery, tactics and ethos came to be about destroying enemy ships whenever and wherever possible. Duelling at a distance made no sense… It was this ethos that made the Royal Navy what it was, the ethos which contributed to the construction of empire, the growth of trade, the globalisation of industry.

The fleet became the Royal Navy after the restoration of the monarchy via Charles the Second in 1660 and formalised its man-to-man fighting force, the Royal Marines. In 1853, impressment, which had many colourful tales of 'recruits' finding themselves on board and now sailors after a heavy night's drinking, was made obsolete when continuous service was introduced by which men could make a life in the navy a career and earn a pension at the end of it.

John 'Jacky' Fisher became First Sea Lord in 1904 and occupied the position for six years, embarking on a period of revolution during this time. The stock of ships was ageing and he scrapped many of them, retiring ninety obsolete warships and placing an additional sixty-four into reserve, describing them as 'a miser's hoard of useless junk,' and 'too weak to fight and too slow to run away'. But the most radical step was the conception and building of the 'all-big-gun' and steam turbine propelled battleships starting in 1906 with *Dreadnought*. With its ten twelve-inch guns, this vessel immediately made all existing battleships obsolete. The design was so revolutionary that all similar warships were also called Dreadnoughts and the introduction of this new warship resulted in an arms race between Britain and Germany.

As is often the case in history, small events can lead to large consequences. Napoleon at Waterloo, and Lee at Gettysburg, both disappeared from the battlefield for a time due to digestive problems. It can even be argued that the Great War was a result of a choice of sandwiches and faulty navigation. Gavrilo Princip, who shot Archduke Franz Ferdinand and his wife, is reported to have decided on some food from Schiller's delicatessen in Sarajevo after a first unsuccessful attempt at assassination. As he emerged, the Archduke's car was reversing after taking a wrong turn. He couldn't believe his luck and opened fire. Six weeks later, World War One started. Clearly, another spark, sometime, somewhere, would have started hostilities, but if Princip had chosen ham instead of cheese, it might have taken a minute longer (or less) to make, and he might have been gone before the Archduke stopped outside…

Kaiser Wilhelm had, in pre-war days, observed the English fleet at close quarters, and attended regattas where he became envious of British sailing prowess. By 1914, the British Navy had nineteen Dreadnoughts (thirteen under construction), compared with Germany's thirteen (seven under construction). The reduced reserve fleet was made more ready for war and inshore duties were taken over by the new surface and submarine flotillas concentrated to meet the threat posed by this growing German High Seas Fleet. In 1908, Fisher predicted, with brilliant foresight, that war between Britain and Germany would begin in October 1914, which later proved accurate. He was basing his statement on the projected completion date of the Kiel Canal, which Germany needed to move its warships safely from the Baltic to the North Sea. After continuous clashes with Lord Beresford, who commanded the Channel Fleet, he retired in 1910.

In 1914, Winston Churchill, now in charge of the Admiralty, recalled Fisher to office as First Sea Lord. In November, 1914, two British armoured cruisers were sunk off the coast of Chile by the superior German East Asiatic Squadron. Controversially, Fisher ordered the despatch of two battle cruisers from the British Grand Fleet to the South Atlantic. His gamble paid off at the Battle of the Falkland Islands on 8th December, 1914, when the German raiders were destroyed.

The only major battle in the Great War between the two navies was off the coast of Jutland (to the Germans 'Skagerrak') on May 31st and June 1st, 1916. Unfortunately for the Germans, British Naval intelligence had broken their code and was aware of its enemy's intentions. On the afternoon of May 31st, a combined force of two hundred and fifty ships collided in an epic duel that lasted through the darkness of night and ended when, under cover of that darkness, the German fleet escaped to its home port to lick its wounds and repair both ships and men.

In the afternoon of the 31st, two German groups under Admiral Scheer were heading north whilst Admiral Beatty with the British battle cruisers was heading east and Admiral Jellicoe with the Grand Fleet was behind him and steaming south east. The German strategy was based on their submarines intercepting the British battle cruisers of 5th Squadron, but the British Grand Fleet had managed to elude the submarines and because of bad weather preventing Zeppelins flying reconnaissance missions, Scheer had no idea what he was about to run into.

By chance, a neutral merchant vessel was steaming along the line of advance of both fleets. Her smoke was sighted almost simultaneously by both sides, who sent cruisers to investigate, upon which each realised the situation. Again, small events had big consequences. It was unlucky for the British that the fleets met in this way; had the commercial ship not been in the area the combatants would almost certainly have met later and the German High Seas Fleet would have been that much further from home.

It was the British plan to cut off a German retreat by positioning itself between the German Fleet and its home ports. It was unfortunate for Beatty that the ships of his 5th Battle Squadron failed to get the signal to attack, and continued on toward a predetermined meeting with Jellicoe and the rest of the fleet for several precious minutes. Thus Beatty's battle cruisers were head on to meet the Germans in relatively close combat. This was not what these ships were designed to do, and they paid dearly for the mistake. When the exchanges took place the British lost the HMS *Queen Mary* and the battle cruiser HMS *Indefatigable* with nearly all men on board, while the battle cruiser HMS *Lion* suffered heavy damage. The 5th Battle Squadron eventually turned around and now had the Germans outgunned, but Scheer was approaching from the south with his main fleet. This forced Beatty to withdraw north and started the second phase of the battle.

Ships on both sides were damaged and sunk, but the British Grand Fleet fared by far the best. After ten minutes, Scheer had had enough and ordered his ships to retire from battle, performing an abrupt turn and disappearing through clouds of smoke and the gathering dusk in order to escape. After ten minutes, at around 7 pm, he turned his ships around again, this time a hundred and eighty degrees, hoping to pass by the rear of the British line. Unfortunately for him, Jellicoe had guessed his course of action correctly and was able to bring the Germans under fire once again. The British were able to score hits on the Germans without sustaining any damage to themselves. More German ships were damaged, but a German torpedo attack, although it scored no hits, distracted the British battle line long enough for Scheer to distance himself from Jellicoe.

As darkness fell, Jellicoe was still between Scheer and Germany and the German battle cruisers were still being punished by Beatty. Scheer ordered his force of six pre-Dreadnoughts (built before the Dreadnought class was conceived) to come to the aid of the battle cruisers by covering their escape from Beatty. The battle continued spasmodically through the night and several ships on both sides were lost; when the Germans sank the British cruiser Black Prince, the way was open to safety.

Thus ended the Battle of Jutland, and both sides returned to their respective home ports. Both claimed to have won the battle.

The British lost more men than the Germans, with six thousand and ninety-four men perishing against the German's two thousand five hundred and fifty-one, and more ships – fourteen against eleven. There were reasons. In order to defeat the British Navy, Germany needed to destroy a large number of British ships. In this, she ultimately failed. After the Grand Fleet returned to Scapa Flow, Jellicoe telegraphed the Admiralty that he could be ready to sail at four hours' notice, his battleships having survived the battle unscathed. Scheer's fleet was in need of serious repair and would not be ready for action again for several months. In fact, Germany never again challenged the Grand Fleet in open battle, preferring instead to switch its emphasis to submarine operations, at which she enjoyed some measure of success.

With the British ships there was a construction defect. The turrets were designed in such a way that a shell could penetrate the turret and start a fire in the ammunition handling rooms which could easily spread to the magazine. The fire would then, of course, blow up the ship. HMS Lion was, in fact, damaged this way and was only saved from total destruction by the heroism of a dying man who managed to close the door that led to the magazine. The German ships originally had this defect too but had corrected it after a skirmish at Dogger Bank, also in the North Sea.

Additionally, as suggested above, the British battle cruisers weren't really used in the proper manner. These warships were designed to go fast and to fire their huge guns from a long distance away. When used properly they could be deadly, because their guns could fire at ranges that were outside the range of their prey's smaller weapons.

Earlier in the war, at the aforementioned Battle of the Falkland Islands, there was a perfect example of battle cruiser tactics. Germany lost four out of five marauding raiders, the British none. The battle cruiser *Invincible* was one of the victorious participants, but she went down with all hands at Jutland. So there is a question as to why the British attacked the enemy the way they did at Jutland and why Beatty moved towards the enemy when he knew his guns had a longer range and the main British force was in close proximity.

One of Britain's goals was to relieve the blockade of Russia in the Baltic Sea. This too, was not achieved, but the threat of the German High Seas Fleet was removed, the German fleet sitting idle for the rest of the war. Britain continued to rule the waves.

Frank Clarke, of Providence House, Arkholme, the son of a railway signalman, also served in the Royal Navy. Like many of his contemporaries in the area, he had become a farm worker after leaving school. As with Bertie Hainsworth and in the next generation, the Newby brothers, he must have wanted to see the world; he saw the world war.

By 1914, the Pearsons had long been a family of note in the south-east of the old county of Westmorland. The names Francis and Fenwick run through the family and it was a surgeon with those Christian names that bought a medical practice in Kirkby Lonsdale in 1780. A later Francis Fenwick was known as 'The Poor Man's Lawyer' for his commendable habit of defending (usually successfully) those who had limited financial resources. Relatives included a rear admiral, Sir Richard, and a surgeon, Alexander, who carried out the first trepanning operation in (the north of) England. The patient had suffered a head injury through a horse carriage turning over and Alexander lifted a lump of skull to relieve the pressure; he was rewarded with a gold watch and the patient with an extended life.

Towards the middle of the nineteenth century, Francis Fenwick Pearson married an Ann Bagot and they had three sons, one a Francis, who bought Gressingham Hall in about 1844 and built the radical Steps in Kirkby Lonsdale. These climb from the river Lune to what is now called Ruskin's View; that painter called it 'one of the loveliest views in England'. Turner also painted it and his watercolour sold a couple of years ago for just under a quarter of a million pounds. This Francis Pearson also bought Storrs Hall in Arkholme, largely demolishing the existing building started by the Stothers (later Storrs) family and replacing it with one of Gothic design. It is lovely, as the photograph in Chapter Two shows.

Frank Pearson, a descendant of the above, was born at Storrs Hall in 1871 and became a solicitor, like most of the males in his family. Frank served with distinction in the Boer War in the Loyal North Lancashire regiment, almost certainly being under siege at Kimberley for four months during the southern hemisphere summer of late 1899 and 1900. The town was relieved by a force under Sir John French, who led the BEF into Belgium in August 1914.

It is appropriate here to describe the expectations of a British officer such as Frank Pearson or Frank Booth. They have an impact on everything in the Great War and explain some of the losses sustained by those officers. It was the traditional and firm belief of that class of men that they were not only braver than their men but braver than officers in other armies. This was almost certainly true, in the sense that the British officer was expected without question to behave in a certain way, and he just about always did. Byron Farwell in *For Queen and Country* explains why the Victoria Cross became the most difficult of medals to acquire. It was because the standard was so high: 'Officers were expected to remain cool under fire and not to 'bob' – that is, not to duck when bullets whistled close or shells exploded near them. Major-General Arthur Fitzroy Hart was known as 'No Bob' Hart because he never flinched under fire and cursed his men when they did.' General Redvers Buller, Commander in the second Boer War and an extremely courageous but stupid man, ordered his officers to forbid their men from becoming 'Jack in the Boxes,' that is soldiers who jump up and shoot and then duck down again. To the modern soldier, this would seem an excellent strategy. In any case, Buller's bravery wasn't enough; his leadership was a disaster in that war.

As late as 1896 there is written testimony of views bordering on racism and xenophobia. General Osborne Wilkinson wrote: 'The day is still very remote when the warlike races of India will be able to supply (take the place of) the European (British!) officer'. Taken a stage further, the Edwardian class system reared its ugly head in the conduct of the war. Sir John French, Commander of the British Expeditionary Force, commenting on the French generals, told Kitchener: 'They are a low lot, and one always has to remember the class these generals came from'. The result was the paradox of First World War officers coming predominantly from the landed classes, leading with immense courage, and suffering horrendous casualties as a result. Because of that, a form of meritocracy very slowly emerged in the army ranks when those of a different class had to be promoted.

And bravery? Refer to Walter Jackson, George Harrison and the thousands of other 'ordinaries' who won gallantry medals or were cited for courage. It has to be noted that the near sixty thousand dead, wounded or missing on the first day of the Somme didn't include a general, that the 'Other Ranks' had their letters censored by officers whose own missives were assumed to be above any possible editing, and that many 'Tommies' were fighting for a country that didn't allow them to vote.

After the Boer War, Frank Pearson returned to practise law at the family firm of Pearson and Pearson in Kirkby Lonsdale and then in other towns in the north Lancashire/south Westmorland area. April 1911 finds him at the Grand Hotel, London, with his pregnant wife staying at her family's home in Kirkby Lonsdale. The war years then see him back as a captain in his Loyal North Lancs regiment, based at Preston. He didn't survive the war, dying of pneumonia (after, possibly, a much earlier road accident) in a military hospital in Prees Heath in Shropshire in February 1918. After this, the house was regarded as 'unlucky', and was firstly divided up and then rented out to the Booths.

Frank's younger brother Louis was born with a back problem. He was named after his mother, Louisa, who died giving birth to him or shortly after. He went to public school in Rutland and, with Frank, inherited £13,670, about £1,040,000 in today's terms, when his father died in 1910. This is probably why he was described for most of his life as living off 'private means', though he only left £75 to his family's solicitors firm when he died in Torquay in 1944. He joined the Artist's Rifles and went to their training camp at Romford, Essex in July, 1917 but suffered a recurrence of his back problem and returned north to be treated at Lancaster Military Hospital and then at Harrogate. He served as Private Secretary to Arthur Stanley, younger brother to the Lord Derby who instigated the idea of the Pals Battalions. Stanley was M.P. for Ormskirk from 1898 until 1918, provincial Grand Master of the Isle of Man

Freemasons from 1902 to 1912 and Treasurer of St Thomas' Hospital from 1917 to 1943. He was knighted for his services in 1917 and died, unmarried, in 1947.

Politics was always near to hand in the Pearson family of latter years. Louis was a close friend of Herwald Ramsbotham, the First Viscount Soulbury, who became the Member of Parliament for Lancaster, twelve miles from Arkholme, in 1929. Frank Pearson's son - inevitably Francis Fenwick - carried on the political/military tradition. After attending Uppingham public school in Rutland — as Uncle Louis had done — he went abroad and became an officer in the Gurkhas. He had the horrific experience of attempting to intervene in one of the Muslim/Hindu massacres prompted by the partition of India in 1947. In 1959 he was elected as MP for Clitheroe, another Lancashire county town, and was then appointed by the Prime Minister, Alec Douglas-Home, as his private secretary.

Frank Pearson's name is on the plaque in the church in Arkholme. True, he was born there and died in a military hospital and it could have been uncomfortable in the designation of 'Thankful Village' that he is described on a tribute in the church in Gressingham as having given his life for his country during the 1914-1918 conflict. At his funeral in Kirkby Lonsdale, his death was described as being from sickness, and he was clearly regarded as being from that town. George Booth, Frank Booth's father, was in attendance, as was brother Louis. Frank Pearson's grave is in St Mary's churchyard and his name is on the church's memorial, as is that of Fred Murray, who was also born in Arkholme but had left for war from Mitchelgate in the town. He was killed near Ypres in April 1918. Again, he should not really be on the scroll in St John's. (As an aside, the Fenwick Arms, between Nether Kellet and Hornby, is well worth a stop if you are passing by.)

Charles Cyril Crossley of Myrtle Grove, Nether Kellet, joined the Loyal North Lancs regiment in September 1915. He was under age at sixteen. He passed his medical but became ill in early 1917 with some kind of heart murmur and was discharged in April of that year. It was probably as good a 'Blighty' (an injury or health matter, usually a wound that wasn't life threatening but got a soldier back to Britain) as one could get. Charles survived until 1965 and had had a son, Andrew, in 1940, and then Richard in 1953, when he was 54 years of age. He was part of the 14th Battalion formed in June 1915 from Home Service personnel. Based initially at Blackpool, it moved to Witham (Essex) in January 1917. There is no record of it being in Ireland. The significance is that Richard says there is a family tradition that his father was in Cork as a soldier. Now that is pretty specific – not just Ireland, but Cork. The expansion of this significance is below.

In 1919, a sharp depression hit the western world. GDP or gross domestic product (production of goods and services in the country) fell by 10.9% in 1919 and then 6% in the following year. Many ex-servicemen were unemployed, as will be shown in Chapter Nine. In Ireland the quest for independence continued, despite the failed Easter Uprising of 1916. In response the 'Black and Tans' were formed and if the family tradition about Charles Crossley is correct then it seems that he was a recruit of this body of men, who are still a symbol of imperialism in Eire; a 'Tan' is still a term of hatred. Most recruits were ex-soldiers with World War One experience. I quote 'Historyphil' on The Great War Forum:

The Black and Tans were signed up in England in 1920 to be Royal Irish Constabulary (R.I.C.) personnel as Police Constables. They were always intended to be police and should be seen as such even from our distance in time. They had no administrative or other links with the British Army (B.A.) and did not have to have been a member of the Armed Forces to join the

R.I.C. It was simply that more men were wanted as the indigenous [sic] Irish were not joining due to the RIC boycott and resignations from the RIC were seriously affecting its operational effectiveness so a recruitment drive took place in Britain. It was so successful (due to the postwar economic depression) that there were not enough RIC uniforms to go around for the inrush of new recruits and to make them appear official they wore any type or mix of uniform some even wearing WWI 'Hospital blues'. The shortfall of uniforms was soon rectified and very quickly all RIC wore the same dark blue serge material and were bound by the same rules of conduct or were sacked.

The Auxiliaries however were a different formation altogether, officially known as 'Auxiliary, Royal Irish Constabulary' (ADRIC)... the ADRIC recruits were drawn only from men who had previously held officer rank in the B.A. Such was the interest in joining that before they were even considered for enrolment into the ADRIC that war service record was used as a filter system, with the result many held decorations for bravery including 3 Victoria Cross holders. Men of action were required and such were recruited. General Crozier... considered that his men were not bound by consensual policing methods as they were officers and therefore gentlemen consequently he did not exercise any type of discipline on them but they had been required to act as policemen and support the RIC in the 'troubled districts'.

From Day 1 of their formation, the Auxies wore a distinctive style of uniform, of tailored to fit Army Kahaki Jackets displaying military decorations and Sam Browne belts with an open low slung (quick draw) revolver holster, tailored riding breeches and highly polished boots all topped off with Tam o' Shanter hats to mark themselves out, to give a kind of 1920's 'come an' get it if ya think your hard enough' message, very tough individuals whose boyhood had been spent in WWI and with an awful reputation in Ireland that they worked very hard at achieving.

In 1919, the British government advertised for men who were willing to 'face a rough and dangerous task'. Many former British army soldiers had come back from Western Europe and did not find a land fit for heroes. Many came back to unemployment and few firms needed men whose primary skill was fighting in war and whose previous job now had a different incumbent. There were, therefore, plenty of ex-servicemen who were willing to reply to the government's advert. For many the sole attraction was not political or national pride – it was simply money. The men got paid ten shillings a day, and three month's training before being sent to Ireland. The first unit arrived in Ireland in March 1920. One Commander, a Lt. Col. Smyth summed up their attitude:

If a police barracks is burned or if the barracks already occupied is not suitable, then the best house in the locality is to be commandeered, the occupants thrown into the gutter. Let them die there – the more the merrier.

Should the order ('Hands Up') not be immediately obeyed, shoot and shoot with effect. If the persons approaching (a patrol) carry their hands in their pockets, or are in any way suspicious-looking, shoot them down. You may make mistakes occasionally and innocent persons may be shot, but that cannot be helped, and you are bound to get the right parties some time. The more you shoot, the better I will like you, and I assure you no policeman will get into trouble for shooting any man.

At Croke Park in November, 1920, the worst incident took place. In retaliation for the murder of fourteen undercover detectives by the IRA, the Black and Tans opened fire on the crowd, killing twelve people. In retaliation for this attack, eighteen members of the 'Auxies' were killed in Kilmichael, County Cork. The 'Auxies' took their revenge for this by burning down the centre of Cork and parading around after this event with burnt cork in their caps. That may have been where Charles Crossley was; if so, a victim of economic circumstances and a land that turned out not to be fit for heroes, but one where you could earn ten shillings a day for getting back into uniform. And the IRA was as brutal as its opponents, who were only formed because of murders of regular policemen. The basic problem was that Britain shouldn't have been there, but it couldn't, at that time, solve the problem of Ulster.

The Anglo-Irish Treaty of December 1921 brought the conflict to an end but created the ground for the 'Troubles' to come. At the time the Republicans were in serious trouble. The IRA had little ammunition left and the Sinn Fein leadership was urging for negotiation. The Irish people were, on the whole, sick of conflict. The 'Irish Problem' had been a long-standing one and Britain had wanted home rule for the whole of Ireland since 1914, but was fearful for the safety of Ulster Catholics at the hands of the heavily-armed Protestant Unionists.

Either way, don't order a 'Black and Tan' (beer and Guinness) if you find yourself in a Dublin pub; it would be like ordering a 'Stuka divebomber' in a bar in Dunkirk.

Eight Arkholme men and probably one or two Nether Kellet ones (their records are not definitive), plus Fred Bullough, the Headmaster at Over Kellet, joined the Royal Artillery. This body had (though only slowly recognised) become the real element in winning or losing the war. The Arkholme men were Robert Robinson, Harold Wilson, Walter Newhouse, Walter Thompson, Bill and Tom Williamson and Thomas and John Ireland. The other Ireland brother, William, was in his local regiment, the King's Own. Like many of the Ireland family, he was a basket maker. In their book *The Somme*, Australian historians Wilson and Prior sum up the battle:

In fact, the British infantry, when they were adequately supported by firepower – the factor that was the determination of victory on the Western

Front – could perform as well as their enemy; if fire support was adequate a well-trained division could exercise its skill and capture its objectives. If such support was absent a Maxse, Tudor or Walker (successful generals) could make no difference whatever.

One of our men, though he started as a gunner, joined the Machine Gun Corps and finished up in a different trade, as a saddler. Thomas Williamson, the son of Thomas and Jane (née Garlick) joined the Royal Field Artillery in 1915; his stated profession was postman. He then transferred to the Royal Garrison Artillery (the really big, semi-stationary guns) and then the Machine Gun Corps. He finished up in Egypt after illness or injury and when he was returned to home in March 1919 he was given an exemplary report. Like many ideal soldiers, however he had a blot on his record, being docked seven days' pay for 'lack of attention on parade' when lining up at Grantham's training camp in May 1917. Perhaps he needed the two policewomen (see Chapter Seven) to make him concentrate!

The artillery consisted basically of two types, guns and howitzers. The former fired AT the enemy in a flat trajectory whilst the latter fired upwards in a parabolic curve, aiming to land the bigger shell ON the enemy. The Great War's static character led to a tendency for bigger non-mobile howitzers, leading to the massive casualties among the infantry. Some could fire one-ton shells six miles, reaching a height four times higher than Mount Snowdon; the impact of its landing can only be imagined. The sixty pounder could fire up to five miles.

Each type of gun and each projectile made a different sound and (if seen) variations of flashes. Mentally it was a horror for the targeted troops. The sounds varied from that of a professional hitting a golf ball or a piece of cloth being torn to a steam train running through an empty station. The troops became so familiar with them that they gave names to some. A 'Jack Johnson' was the British nickname used to describe the impact of a heavy, black German 15cm artillery shell, Johnson being the black heavyweight champion of the world until cheated out by white racists in 1915. Similarly, a 'Coal Box' was called by that name as a result of it being a high explosive German shell which gave off a heavy black smoke. A German would call this a 'Schwarze Maria' while to a French *poilu* (infantryman) it was a 'Gros Noir'. Stories are told of new recruits ducking at the sound of guns firing whilst old sweats would know from the sound whether danger was imminent; they would carry on with what they were doing as the shell sailed overhead.

The gunners' skills developed into an art form, linking up with the developing radio communication (remember Frank Booth and Arthur Graham's military careers) and mastering dial sights, field clinometers, fuse settings, elevation levels and other dark practices that enabled them to hit targets they couldn't see.

One tactic slowly adopted by the artillery was that of the 'creeping barrage'. First used on the Eastern Front, it was suggested in April 1916 by Rawlinson prior to the Somme. In his 'Tactical Notes' he suggested: 'The ideal is for the artillery to keep their fire immediately in front of the infantry as the latter advances, battering down all opposition with a hurricane of projectiles'. Few instances occurred on the first day of the Somme except in the southern sector, where the French partially employed it to good effect or not in a comprehensive way as in front of Fricourt and Montauban. Some success was still achieved in these places. As the practice of this type of artillery attack developed and the skills of the gunners improved as described above, the creeping barrage became very effective. By November the following principles had been laid down in operation orders: 'The leading infantry should follow so closely on the heels of the barrage that the enemy has no time to recover or man his machine guns before they are upon him'. Our Lunesdale men would have been subject to these new skills and the resultant proficiencies; nevertheless their relationship with the infantry must have been like a knife thrower and his assistant pinned to the rotating disc.

In Nether Kellet, future artillery men Charles Bibby and his two years younger brother John were living at Bank House when war broke out. After the war, Charles became a bank clerk and lived into his seventies. Edward Bradshaw was at Dixon's Terrace and Christopher Orr at Jubilee Terrace. Benjamin Stout Corless joined the Loyal North Lancs and was in the company of a number of Lunesdale men; it's possible he was trained by Cpt Frank Pearson. Benjamin married in the early twenties and died in Garstang in 1941.

Richard Herbert Robinson and his brothers Clifford and Arthur were the sons of William and Agnes, the former a housepainter from Cramlington in Northumberland. That town would later see one of the incidents of the 1926 General Strike when the striking miners attempted to put a stop to 'blackleg' coal being rushed through the village by train; they dismantled the rail track in broad daylight. They only managed to derail the next train, which happened to be the Flying Scotsman, which, as well as regular passengers was carrying strikebreakers. Two people were injured and the offenders got between four and eight years in prison.

The Robinsons had originally moved to Poulton-le-Sands, one of three villages that made up Morecambe, but they had then relocated to Nether Kellet and in 1911 were living at Dunald Mill, near one of the local quarries. The building still stands today. Effort has been made to piece their history together, but as Arthur was under age it has proven difficult. We cannot match up the three brothers to the same regiment, as is sometimes the case. It seems that the Robinsons had two more children, Agnes, named after her mother, and Joseph. The latter, and Arthur, served in the Second World War.

John Thomas Harrison lived at Town End, Nether Kellet, and had three sons, George Edwin, John Thomas (Jack) and William; all three are on the St Mark's plaque of returners. George is remembered as a very kind man. He lived at Bank House next to the school, his house having a barn; amongst the implements in there were some sledges. When it snowed the children were let out of classes to play in the field opposite and the sledges would appear as if by magic! What would Health and Safety say now? William was sadly killed in an accident in the village when a local farmer unwittingly pinned him against a wall with some farm machinery.

John had two sons, Jack and Dennis, who served in World War Two in the RAF and Royal Engineers respectively. Their names are on the plaque as World War Two returners in this Doubly Thankful village.

George Pollock and his younger sibling John were the sons of the Headmaster and Headmistress of the village school. Andrew and Sarah Pollock had arrived from Sunderland, the former being the son of a ship's joiner. It is likely that George was in the Royal Artillery (two similar men fit the bill) like his six neighbours from Arkholme and that John joined him. The school was called Bateson Memorial after Elizabeth Bateson, who, as a seventeen-year-old in the 1860s, would walk up from Bolton-le-Sands to give a Sunday School. The project developed until the room she was using became too small and her brother bought her a house and a barn with a plot of land; soon the barn was a Sunday school in the morning, a place of worship in the afternoon and a night school on three evenings a week. It progressed to be a day school and a Congregational Church had been built on the land by the time of

Elizabeth's death in 1900. The Education Department now demanded a bigger school and land to build it on was offered and sold by Septimus Booker, the father of Gerald and Rowland of Over Kellet (Chapter Six). That schoolmaster's house became Bateson Memorial House, occupied by the Pollock family on the outbreak of war in 1914.

Most, if not all, of the soldiers who fought in World War One and returned to the village would have attended the school. They would have had their hair combed back, their faces polished shiny, and been encased in their best clothes for their Sunday school. It would little have dawned on them what they would go through and the return they would make. Perhaps while on the Western Front some would attend Toc H (a clergyman's property, organised to give soldiers away from the line a window of peace and refuge) in Poperinghe, Flanders, and in a moment of tranquillity think of the quiet Sunday afternoons in Nether Kellet.

Bateson Memorial House

William Stott lived three doors away from Walter Jackson in Nether Kellet. He must have been influenced by him, as he joined the King's Own and also became a sniper. His granddaughter Marion Preston remembers him some time after the war as being interested in local football and being told that he had to change his job to work in a local quarry when the ironworks where he was employed in Carnforth closed in 1929. He had worked as a furnace man there and then transferred his skills to the quarry job. Bill had got married on Christmas Day 1915 and joined up with his regiment the following February, going to France in May 1917. Like many of the men who came back, as stated above, he didn't talk about the war. It seems likely that he was wounded or suffered illness as he moved to the Royal Army Service Corps in March 1918. He died in 1965.

We are now left with a small number of men who went to war, returned, and carried on with their lives, usually in a fairly unspectacular way. That does not diminish them in any way whatsoever. Being human beings they would have mainly lived decent lives, raising families and looking after them and their friends and neighbours. They would have sometimes lost tempers, sometimes told untruths and often just the truth. They would have thanked God for their survival and return, would have berated Him for the loss of family or comrades, or would have wondered as to His existence or not. Some would have told tales of the war but most would have let it just fade away. Nightmares of things seen would have given restless nights and wounds, real and mental, might have faded for some. All would have hoped for what later came to be written on the Nether Kellet Stone: A Lasting Peace. They never got it.

The following, in some cases, should have the words 'almost certainly', 'probably' or 'seems likely' as a prefix to their description. Over half of the records of men of the First War were, ironically, destroyed by bombing in the Second War. I have used other sources such as probate, newspapers and verbal testimony where possible.

There is no trace of Braithwaite Hayton on any records; the plaque in St John's is clear that he was in the 1st Lifeguards, so we must take that as read. Richard Williamson, brother to the siblings described earlier in the chapter, also entered this unit. The conclusion is that as Braithwaite had just turned fifteen when war broke out (living at Bainsbeck, Arkholme) he must have used a false name when volunteering. Did he and Richard go to the Lifeguards together? Almost certainly; Richard was two years older and familiar with horses, as testified by his father's occupation on a farm and his brothers' proficiencies, one as a wheelwright and the other as a saddler. The Lifeguards were a mounted unit that was used in royal guard and ceremonial events as well as active duties. Perhaps the equine character attracted him, but in March 1918, the Lifeguards were converted to a machine gun battalion. In passing, and to add to the comments in Chapter Seven, we can derive a description from Jonty Wilson's *A Cumbrian Blacksmith*. He wrote that the horses suffered when in France, becoming neglected when the cavalrymen were sent to the front to supplement the infantrymen. Just one man was left behind to look after eight horses 'to feed, clean and exercise... an impossible task.'

Braithwaite married Marjorie Ireland, the daughter of Mark, the sub-postmaster and previous next-door neighbour of Bertie Hainsworth. He survived into his nineties, still at Bainsbeck where his family still live today and run a wagon repair workshop. His younger brother Cecil married another Ireland, Beatrice, daughter of John the artilleryman described above. Cecil became a World War Two combatant, survivor and returner. A.E. Allonby, like many of his peers, served in the local regiment, the King's Own. William Simon (or Simm) Holme was born in Kendal and lived in Arkholme for a period of his life but was living on Main Street, Kirkby Lonsdale, in 1911. He might have felt an affiliation further north, as he joined the Border Regiment in the war; he was 42 years of age when war broke out.

Tom Bownass, the son of Richard and Margaret Ann, was brought up at Docker Park and moved to Lancaster to work in a silk mill. He enlisted just before Christmas 1914, joining the Duke of Wellington's West Riding Regiment. He married Mary Hutton Casson in Settle in 1920 and moved to Ewecross, right on the West Riding/Lancashire border, where he died in 1970. William Hornby was a very common name in the King's Own and Cumberland and Westmorland Regiments and the only one we could trace died at Arras in 1918. We have to assume he wasn't our man. There are two Ralph Bibbys; the one that later fought with the Cumberland and Westmorland Regiment was born in Tatham, near Lancaster and was there in 1911; if it is him on the Arkholme scroll, his connection with the village is unclear.

James Birkett Huddlestone was born in Arkholme on the last day of January, 1884. He learned the Arkholme trade of basket weaving but had moved to Birmingham and was practising that trade there in 1911, four years after marrying Emily Tunnicliffe in Lichfield, and they had four children before the war. He joined the local Warwickshire Regiment and at the end of the war returned to Birmingham to become a pub landlord. His wife gave birth to twins in 1920, but both died at birth and Emily passed away a year later. James married again in 1925 and passed away in Birmingham in 1950.

Brothers William, Joseph and Albert Rumney were all in the East Lancashire Regiment, famed for its Accrington Pals, Albert joining up under age, as he was born in 1900. The families lived in Chapel Houses, Lancaster Road and had a tradition of working on railway construction, though Joseph had moved to Garstang by 1911 to work at a farm. After the war he and Albert moved to Bolton, where Albert died in 1922. He married twice, his first wife dying in 1928, and passed away in Farnworth, near Bolton, in 1940.

Thomas Edgar Buncle was Scottish, having been born in Forfar, Arbroath, in 1896. It seems he came south with his mother who was a Headmistress in Claife, near Windermere, but was originally from Ulverston. He joined the RAF and was in Arkholme at some stage after the war; then, like Bertie Hainsworth, he joined the Merchant Navy. Perhaps he was in the village between spells on board ship. It is thought that he returned to Scotland.

Harry Dodding was born in Arkholme on Christmas Eve, 1894. His mother Agnes died when he was seven, and his father Bill when he was fourteen. By 1911 he was split up from his brother and sister, all three working separately as servants in one form or another. He joined the Seaforth Highlanders and must have received a wound, as he finished the war in the Labour Corps. He died in Lancaster in 1972.

John Carr Bownass, who got the Carr part of his name from his mother's surname, was the son of Edward, who ran Cort's farm in Arkholme. John was clearly pretty bright and became an architect's draughtsman. He joined the Royal Army Medical Corps. After the war he survived only until August 1920 ('flu?) and left his savings to an older lady; the probate says Dora Sproat, who was forty-one at the time. She married a Robert Boyd in Kendal in 1919, so she would have been Dora Boyd at the time of John's death. No, I don't understand either.

John Wilson, Arthur Bownass and Frank Webster all joined the Royal Engineers. John was the son of a coal merchant and brother to Harold, who was an artilleryman. Frank was the son of the Headmaster at Stainton, Cumbria, and he was in the village in 1911; his brother George was with the Bibby family in Arkholme.

George Victor Croft was in the Wiltshire Regiment; before the war he was working on the Steels' farm in Heysham and obviously made an impression – he married the farmer's daughter Ellen in 1916.

Albert Lawson may well have been illegitimate as he is with John Ducket Lawson at Broomfield, Arkholme, in 1901 and 1911, but is described as grandson in the first census and then nephew in the second. His mother was probably Mary, John Ducket's daughter. Albert joined the Lancashire Fusiliers and received a wound or became ill as he finished up in the Labour Corps, like many others in this testimony. He married Jessie Townley of Lancaster in 1920, and he died in 1940; Jessie remarried two years later. George Sedgwick is another King's Own man. Again, he was fifteen or sixteen when war broke out and may have lied about his age. He died in 1969. His younger brother Harry was born just after the First War and died during the Second; he was living in Over Kellet and is commemorated on their memorial.

Thomas Mason, shown as Mason Thomas on the church scroll (so that's why we couldn't find him!) was another man of farming stock, giving his occupation on his attestation papers as 'farmer and horseman'. He was working at Snab Green in 1914, though his parents had only just moved there from Ingleton and returned there after the war. He died in 1968.

Tom Read was another horseman, living and working at Bonfire Hall, Underbarrow, in 1911. It seems he married Alice Smith and at some stage moved to live with his son Thomas in Todmorden on the Lancashire/Yorkshire boundary, where he died in 1965.

The author has striven to do justice to these men; I hope I have succeeded.

CHAPTER NINE

THE END OF THE WAR, AND AFTER

'Now that I've seen what war is… I know that everybody, if one day it should end, ought to ask himself: 'And what shall we make of the fallen? Why are they dead?' I wouldn't know what to say. Not now, at any rate. Nor does it seem to me that the others know. Perhaps only dead know, and only for them is the war really over' – Cesare Pavese, The House On The Hill.

In the early hours of Monday, 11th November, 1918, four representatives each of the Allies and Germany filed into dining car number 241D of the Wagons-Lits Company in a clearing in the forest of Compiègne, fifty miles north east of Paris. The Great War was about to be ended. The chief German negotiator – though he had nothing to negotiate about – was Matthias Erzberger, a former teacher and future chief scapegoat for the German surrender. Now a politician, he knew he had to do his duty but he also knew that millions of his fellow countrymen, including a Corporal Hitler, at the time blinded and in a hospital in Pasewalk, near the Baltic coast, would never forgive him.

Opposite him and his co-delegates were Marshall Ferdinand Foch, Admiral Rosslyn Wemyss, General Maxime Weygand (charged with enemy collaboration by de Gaulle after World War Two) and Rear Admiral George Hope. The allies asked for utterly punitive concessions, including the handover of over two thousand planes, ten thousand lorries and thirty thousand machine guns. Germany would also give back tracts of land including Alsace/Lorraine, gained in the Franco-Prussian war of 1870. As the Great British economist John Maynard Keynes would point out that this principle of making the Germans pay, confirmed at Versailles the following year, would result in another war somewhere down the line. But on this autumn day, at 11 o clock in the morning, the armistice would come into place and the war would end.

Around twenty-one years later, in the early evening of June 22nd, 1940, Adolf Hitler and his crew of criminals, including Joachim von Ribbentrop, Walther von Brauchitsch, Hermann Göring and Rudolf Hess sat in the same carriage in the same place and witnessed the effective surrender of France to Germany. The carriage had been removed from a museum building and placed on the precise spot where it was located in 1918, and Hitler chose to sit in the same seat Foch had occupied when he faced Erzberger and company in 1918. After listening to the reading of the preamble, Hitler, in a calculated gesture of disdain to the French delegates, left the carriage, as Foch had done in 1918, abandoning the negotiations to the High Commander of the Armed Forces, General Wilhelm Keitel. Much had happened in the two decades separating the two surrenders in that carriage at Compiègne.

Back to November 11th, 1918. Some one hundred and twenty miles to the south-east from that rail car at Compiègne, and an hour and a half from the start of the armistice, Private Henry Gunther of the 313th Infantry was unaware of its existence. A drafted, reluctant soldier, Gunther had been promoted to sergeant as a result of his ability to organise supplies. He had written home advising a friend to keep clear of the army, as the conditions on the Western

Front were so awful. A censor had spotted this comment and as a result he had been demoted to private. Gunther was determined to return to Baltimore as a sergeant rather than a private.

Just before 11 o clock, he found himself, with his friend Ernest Powell, ten miles north of Verdun in front of the village of Ville-devant-Chaumont and a defended ridge just behind it. They were put under intensive fire from the Prussian 31st regiment on the hill. At one minute to eleven, Gunther leapt to his feet and charged. Ernie Powell tried to stop him, and the Germans, aware of the imminent armistice, tried to wave him back. A burst from a machine gun knocked him back; he was the last American to die in the war.

Just ten minute before this, private George Ellison from Leeds was sitting astride his horse on a patch of ground just outside of Mons, when he was hit by a sniper and killed. He was the last British fatality, shot close to where the war had started for the British B.E.F., of which he was a part. An army regular before the war, he had somehow got through the four years, witnessing the Somme and Ypres battles after experiencing the retreat from Mons, the place, ironically where he met his fate.

Just over four miles to the north-east, Private George Lawrence Price from Nova Scotia was part of an advance party tasked to take the small village of Havré. After crossing a bridge over the Canal du Centre, Price and his patrol moved toward a row of houses to find a machine gunner who had been firing on them as they negotiated the canal. He and four colleagues entered the house from where the shooting had come, but just missed their quarry as the Germans had escaped through the back door as Price and his patrol entered the front. They tried the adjoining house with the same result. As George Price stepped back into the street a single shot rang out and he was thrown to the floor. At 10:58 am, Private

Price became the last soldier from Britain and her dominions to perish in the war.

The Saint-Symphorien military cemetery is located a mile or so east of Mons on the N90, a road leading to Charleroi. There, by extraordinary coincidence, lie the first and last British soldiers to die in the war, as well as the last soldier from Britain's dominions. Sixteen-year-old John Parr of Finchley, North London, a golf caddy who lied about his age, is in grave 1A10. George Ellison is in 1B23 and George Price, reinterred after the war, is in VC4. They are buried under pine trees, a few yards apart.

Private First Class Augustin-Joseph Trébuchon was the last Frenchman to die in the war. Forty years of age and a long way from his home in Languedoc, the former shepherd and 1914 volunteer was making for the French lines along the River Meuse in the Ardennes with an 'important message'. Again, he was killed with a single sniper's shot. The message read: 'Muster at 11:30 for food'.

He was the last 'Mort pour la France' in this war.

The author has scoured the library to find the identity of the last German to die in the conflict. There is no clear answer. One story is that a German officer was killed in the Ardennes by American soldiers unaware of the armistice. If so, he was one of four thousand from both sides that were killed that morning.

As described earlier in the book, nineteen mines were blown under the Messines Ridge in midsummer 1917. The explosions were reputed to have been heard in Downing Street and they had a precursor in the mines exploded at the Somme in the previous year. Nine years later the miners who had dug the tunnels – at least, the ones who survived – were totally at odds with the British Government. In February 1915, eight tunnelling companies had been created and were operational in Flanders from March of that year. By mid-1916, the British Army had around twenty-five thousand trained tunnellers, mostly volunteers taken from coal mining communities and 'clay-kickers' who built the London Underground and the Manchester sewage system. The tunnels and the vaults where the explosive ammonal was stacked were dug by miners with accents which would have been from Scotland, London, the north-east, Lancashire, Yorkshire, Nottinghamshire, Kent and Wales; and some French. Some were recruited from infantry battalions, others direct from civilian life. Almost twice that number of 'attached infantry' worked permanently alongside the trained miners, acting as 'beasts of burden'. From the spring of 1917, the whole war became more mobile, and the tactics and counter-tactics required deeper and deeper tunnelling. More stable front lines were also required, meaning that offensive and defensive military mining largely ceased.

Deeper underground excavation continued, with the tunnellers concentrating on deep dugouts for troop accommodation and jump-off points, a tactic used particularly in the battles of Arras and Vimy Ridge. On June 19th 2010, at Givenchy in the Pas de Calais, a tunnellers' memorial was unveiled that sits above the spot where the bodies of William Hackett VC and Thomas Collins still lie. They had to be abandoned after the Germans exploded a mine under the British line on 22nd of June, 1916, and the underground gallery the British were working in collapsed. Five miners were initially interred, but three of them were rescued. Tom Collins had broken ribs and couldn't crawl, and Bill Hackett stayed with him in anticipation of the rescue hole and tunnel being widened. Sadly, a further collapse entombed the pair and they could never be rescued. Their story was not untypical. A few miles away John Lane, 45, and Ezekiel Parkes, 37, were caught in a similar incident; their bodies were never recovered.

At home, the Government had sequestered the coalmines in

1916, and then paid the miners relatively well. The problem was that they volunteered, as in most other industries, in large numbers. A scan through the Great War Forum gives particular information. John Duncan informs the readers:

Miners joined up in huge numbers, causing severe labour shortage in the mines. There were several reports of very young boys (14 or so) and old men of 70 or over being hurt down the pit. Over 80% of the 8th Royal Scots (Pioneers) were miners, which was partly the reason they became Pioneers. My Great Uncle William enlisted in 1916 as a tunneller and he had a letter from the pit manager and the local mining board, but this was primarily to get his 5 bob a day tunneller's pay.

'Wdragon' responds that that South Wales miners who enlisted in the early war period 'were required to have the signature of the mine manager authorising them to go on their enlistment papers before the enlistment centre would accept them and that there were several instances of men enlisting after forging the manager's signature'. Graham Stewart from Darlington comments that local North East papers give accounts of how the mining industry was 'virtually left with only boys and old men with which to extract coal for the war effort'.

The German offensive of spring, 1918, introduced a facet of warfare not seen since the autumn of 1914 – mobility. The effect of a different kind of fighting was remarkable. The Americans had declared war on Germany in April 1917 after a resumption of the sinking of any sea vessels – including those from the USA – suspected of carrying supplies to Great Britain. The sinking of the American liner *Housatonic* by a German U-boat was the last straw for President Wilson and Congress and the country entered the fray. Troops from the USA started to arrive in summer and autumn of that year, but the Germans knew that a deluge was due in 1918. On the Eastern Front, Russia and Germany had made peace after the Revolution of October and this in turn released thousands of German troops for the Western Front. At the same time, the British blockade was seriously damaging the German economy. The Germans had to win the war in 1918.

On March 21st 1918, the offensive - 'Kaiserschlacht' or 'the Emperor's Battle' (he himself was nowhere near) - began. In the first few hours the Germans fired one million artillery shells at the British lines, that's over a hundred and fifty thousand shells an hour, this being followed by an attack by elite storm troopers. These soldiers travelled light and had been trained in fast, hard-hitting attacks, leaving the 'mopping up' to their comrades behind them and moving on to their next target. Unlike soldiers burdened with weighty kit, like the Tommies' 61 pounds, the storm troopers carried little except weaponry (such as flamethrowers) that could cause much panic and fear.

By the end of the first day of the attack, twenty-one thousand British soldiers had been taken prisoner and the Germans had made great advances through the lines of the Fifth Army. Senior British military commanders lost control of the situation. They had spent three years used to static warfare and suddenly they had to cope with a German onslaught of movement and speed. General Gough ordered the Fifth Army to withdraw. The German attack was the biggest breakthrough in three years of warfare on the Western Front and their advance also put Paris in the firing line, using the 'Big Bertha' howitzer. Over one hundred and eighty huge shells landed on the capital and many Parisians left for safer places.

The first few days of the attack were such an overwhelming success that the Kaiser declared March 24th to be a national holiday. Many in Germany assumed that the war was all but over.

On April 11th, it seems that Haig thought the same. He issued the following:

SPECIAL ORDER of the Day
By FIELD-MARSHAL SIR DOUGLAS HAIG K.T., G.C.B.,
G.C.V.O., K.C.I.E
Commander-in-Chief, British Armies in France
To ALL RANKS OF THE BRITISH ARMY IN FRANCE AND
FLANDERS

Three weeks ago to-day the enemy began his terrific attacks against us on a fifty-mile front. His objects are to separate us from the French, to take the Channel Ports and destroy the British Army.

In spite of throwing already 106 Divisions into the battle and enduring the most reckless sacrifice of human life, he has as yet made little progress towards his goals.

We owe this to the determined fighting and self-sacrifice of our troops. Words fail me to express the admiration which I feel for the splendid resistance offered by all ranks of our Army under the most trying circumstances.

Many amongst us now are tired. To those I would say that Victory will belong to the side which holds out the longest. The French Army is moving rapidly and in great force to our support.

There is no other course open to us but to fight it out. Every position must be held to the last man: there must be no retirement. With our backs to the wall and believing in the justice of our cause each one of us must fight on to the end. The safety of our homes and the Freedom of mankind alike depend upon the conduct of each one of us at this critical moment.

The author would argue that 'to the last man' and 'to the end' are not phrases of a man on the verge of a victory, though the communiqué has his usual concept of the winner being the side with the last man standing.

The Germans, however, experienced one major problem. Their advance had been a major success, but as indicated, their troops deliberately carried few things except weapons to assist their mobility. Their supply lines were too long; there are even stories of them coming across wine vaults, with inevitable consequences. Ludendorff had left a million and half troops on the Eastern Front.

The tide turned. Foch was appointed commander of all Allied forces in France and in July initiated a counter-offensive against the Marne salient, eliminating it by August. A second major offensive was launched two days after the first, ending at Amiens to the north. This attack, including the French and British, was spearheaded by Australian and Canadian troops, using six hundred tanks and eight hundred aircraft. The assault proved highly successful for the Allies, leading Hindenburg to name the 8th of August the 'Black Day of the German Army'. By the autumn the war was won.

At the height of the crisis in April, British industry had reacted to the possibility of defeat with a rapid expansion of output. The coal industry led it and epitomised the spirit of the day, with strikes being abandoned or suspended and output shooting up. Other blue-collar workers followed suit, including the munitions industry; the whole of 1918 saw the production of one thousand three hundred and fifty-nine tanks and a staggering one hundred and twenty thousand nine hundred aircraft. In the Clydebank shipyards the men worked through Easter. Recruitment into the army, amazingly, picked up. In Germany, industrial production fell because of the blockade and industrial unrest.

Between the end of the war and 1926, a number of factors had changed the condition of the British coal industry. Other countries had filled the gaps in exports in what were, prior to the war, British markets. Rich seams of coal had been exploited in the conflict, there was a shift to oil in, for example, shipping, Germany came back as a producer in 1924 and our return to the Gold Standard in 1925 raised the price of our exports. The owners were suspected of profiteering during the war, and although they formed associations themselves frowned upon the miners joining unions. A 1919 Royal Commission came out in support of the Government keeping ownership, but as indicated above this was handed back to the private sector in 1921. The owners claimed that the wage rises of the war years were too much and would be lowered, and any miner refusing this would be sacked. The result was a three month lockout in 1921, which the miners lost when the Transport Workers and Railwaymen failed to deliver the support promised. 'Ray', on a Welsh Coal Mines Forum, writes about the lockout: 'Between 1918 and 1921 the miners' wages were the highest in their history and the mines were still under state control. In 1921 the government handed them back to the private owners and they halved the wages. This caused a big strike and lock-out which was particularly vicious at Abertillery, with 250 sailors based in the town. Then trade depressions took place resulting in three of the Abertillery pits, and 2,500 men losing their jobs by 1924'.

The Government supported the owners and sent troops into the coalfields. This was two years after the Peace of Versailles was signed, four since Passchendaele and five since the Somme. Wage cuts of between 10% and 4% were imposed. Further cuts were demanded and the situation came to a head with the General Strike of 1926. There was a victory for the miners on 'Red Friday' in 1925, when the government, not confident that the cuts could be successfully imposed at this point in time, postponed the confrontation. In his report on the industrial situation to the King, Maurice Hankey, Permanent Secretary to the Cabinet, said: 'The majority of the Cabinet regard the present moment as badly chosen for the fight, though the conditions would be more favourable nine months hence.' This was the 'Land Fit For Heroes'.

A nine-month subsidy was given to the coalmining industry and the Samuel Commission was set up to investigate the problems of the industry. The Government began to oversee the stockpiling of coal and made preparations for a confrontation, similar to the situation in 1984. Plans were drawn up for the maintenance of 'order' and recruitment of volunteer strike-breakers. The latter would be handled by the Organisation for Maintenance of Supplies, a 'private' body condemned as neo-fascist by the hardly left wing *Daily Express*.

The government lacked confidence in the Trade Union leaders' ability to control their membership. On October 14th, 1925, the Home Secretary ordered the arrest of eleven leaders of the Communist party, who were subsequently imprisoned for periods of between six and twelve months on charges of seditious libel and incitement to mutiny. The majority were, however, released before the General Strike in May 1926.

The Samuel Commission came up with its 'impartial' findings in early 1926. It reported that there had indeed been mismanagement of the British coalfields, but wage cuts and increased hours were still inevitable in order to make the industry competitive in the world market. So, a full year in which the government prepared for confrontation was lost for the mineworkers. Anger reached boiling point with the results of the commission and the ending of the subsidy. The TUC was forced to call a general strike.

Up to the last minute, the leadership of the TUC attempted to cobble together a deal with the government and made plain their hope that a general strike would be averted. Meanwhile, the British press was busy creating hysteria about the impending class warfare. When printers at the *Daily Mail*, recognisably conservative, went on unofficial strike when asked to publish another anti-union article, the TUC repudiated the action.

On the 4th May 1926, the size and breadth of the General Strike took everyone by surprise, the lead being given at local level. In some areas, embryonic workers' militias formed and violent clashes occurred throughout the country, despite the best attempts of the TUC to maintain a blissful calm. 'Unorganised' workers in some areas were amongst the first to strike and everywhere joined their unionised comrades. Despite efforts by strike-breaking students, the country was coming to a standstill and in many areas little or nothing moved without the agreement of the strikers. The state, for its part, geared up for an escalation, aware of the possibility that things might get 'out of hand'. Battleships were anchored in the Clyde, the Mersey and elsewhere, whilst the army and navy were put on standby, all leave being cancelled. There was a distinct possibility of ex-soldiers and sailors fighting comrades they had shared a trench, deck or wagon with just a few years earlier.

The trade union leaders were anxious to show moderation; one way was via the British Worker. This daily bulletin continually emphasised that the strike was an industrial dispute not political, whilst encouraging local strike committees to organise sports activities and 'entertainments'. Football matches between strikers and the police took place – reminiscent of the 1914 Christmas Truce? Prime Minister Stanley Baldwin described the General Strike as 'a challenge to parliament and the road to anarchy and ruin'. The same man couldn't be bothered even to see a representation from the Jarrow marchers after they had walked the two hundred miles plus to number ten a decade later. He was 'too busy'. At least he didn't want to arm the soldiers, as Churchill advised.

On May 12th, after a period of procrastination and disorganisation, the General Council of the TUC called off the strike. The news, relayed through the British Worker, came as a shock to most strikers and on 13th May there were more workers out than ever before. They were deliberately not told that the mineworkers' union had opposed the ending of the strike and imagined that a victory of some description had been won. Confusion reigned and as news of the capitulation filtered through there was a general sense of bitterness and dockworkers, engineers, railway workers and others continued the strike unofficially.

Eventually, however, the momentum was lost and the workers drifted back to work. The abandoned miners continued their strike officially but were isolated, slowly ground down and defeated. They had helped win one war but then lost another. By the end of the year most were back at work, though many remained unemployed for years. Those that were employed were forced to accept longer hours, lower wages and district wage agreements. It is hard to imagine what the dead tunnellers William Hackett VC and Thomas Collins would have made of it all.

In his wonderful book *Back to The Front*, Stephen O'Shea describes his walk of the whole length of the trenches of the Great War from the English Channel to Switzerland. At one point in the book he talks about his two Irish grandfathers, Daniel O'Shea and Bartholemew Conlon, both Irish and both soldiers of the conflict. He says that after the war they both returned home, Daniel to tailoring in Tralee, Bartholemew to pulling pints in a Dublin pub. Two comments about them are interesting and very relevant. O'Shea says 'their generation must remain a stranger to mine'. Almost everything about the First World War - the way it was fought, the reasons for fighting it, the physical and emotional devastation that followed in its wake - seems almost incomprehensible to us today.

Second, he describes them as being 'discreet to the point of pathological about what they had seen and heard in their years in France'. Daniel died in 1940 and the Dubliner in 1955, but he says that they did not want to talk and neither did we wish to listen. He quotes Michael Ignatieff's statement 'we survivors can mark the spot of their vanished experience and not much else'. Denis Winter in 'Death's Men' confirms the point. He says: 'Men became neither hermits nor criminals but required a period of quietness, a second adolescence as it were, to shed the past and get back into life at a lower key than they were used to. When the vicar of Eye appealed for combat records from his parishioners, he ran into delays of twelve months and was then only given photographs with no particulars. Whilst doing his course at the London Institute of Education, my father noted that nobody ever talked about the past and only by chance did he learn that so-and-so had been a major or staff captain.'

Winter goes on to explain that the mood of celebration was transient. The historian of wartime Leeds noted a 'general desire to forget this horrid war'. In Sunderland, only two thousand of the sixteen thousand soldiers from the area who served attended a reception on Victory Day. No one wanted to see or hear anything to do with the war. Khaki disappeared from the streets as soon as the compulsory twenty-eight day period after demobilisation came to an end. The soldiers counted for less than any generation for three hundred years.

Harry Patch was the last British ex-soldier to pass away, in 2009. He didn't mention the war until he was over a hundred years of age. He talked about it thus:

Opposite my bedroom there is a window and there is a light over the top. Now when the staff go into that room they put the light on. If I was half asleep – the light coming on was the flash of a bomb. That flash brought it all back. For eighty years I've never watched a war film, I never spoke of it, not to my wife. For six years, I've been here [in the nursing home]. Six years it's been nothing but World War One. As I say, World War One is history, it isn't news. Forget it.

The other source of anger was the blood cost. Censorship had deprived people at home of all knowledge of what was going on, though the local newspapers' obituaries (as displayed earlier in this book) did give some semblance as to what was happening. 'Every day one meets saddened women, with haggard faces and lethargic movements,' Beatrice Webb noted in her diary a week after the Armistice, 'and one dare not ask after husband and son'. When the men returned they carried memories with them like Harry Patch's. 'We came across a lad from A company. He was ripped open from his shoulder to his waist by shrapnel and lying in a pool of blood. When we got to him, he said, 'Shoot me'. He was beyond human help and, before we could draw a revolver, he was dead. And the final word he uttered was 'Mother'. I remember that lad in particular. It's an image that has haunted me all my life, seared into my mind.'

He summed up the war:

You used to look between the fire and apertures and all you could see was a couple of stray dogs out there, fighting over a biscuit that they'd found. They were fighting for their lives. And the thought came to me – well, there they are, two animals out there fighting over a dog biscuit, the same as we get to live. They were fighting for their lives. I said, 'We are two civilised nations - British and German - and what were we doing? We were in a lousy, dirty trench fighting for our lives? For what? For eighteen pence a flipping day… politicians who took us to war should have been given the guns and told to settle their differences themselves, instead of organising nothing better than legalised mass murder.

Many participants in the Great War buried painful memories of their experiences of brutality and atrocities. The result was a society paralysed by grief and passive in the face of subsequent fascism, according to historian Annette Becker:

In the old days, when the rules of battle prevailed and soldiers boasted of exploits on the field of glory, stretcher-bearers could expect guns on both sides to pause while they worked. But this evaporated at the Somme in 1916 she adds.. There the wounded - a third of whom might have survived earlier battles - were left to die in the ceaseless carnage.

Becker's book, *1914-1918: Understanding the Great War,* written with Stephane Audoin-Rouzeau, has a subtitle in French: *Retrouver La Grande Guerre.* She prefers the French, as it suggests a re-evaluation, to the English, which possibly claims too much. That is why, Becker says, historians throughout the past eighty years have failed to comprehend it.

In the book she suggests that historians have sidestepped the most painful aspects of the First War; its violence, its atrocities, and its ensuing grief. No killers appear to have returned home, only victims and heroes. She argues that in the 1920s, the war seemed so awful that people started to say they hadn't wanted to be a part of it and just blamed the politicians and the military, claiming they themselves had been against it all the time. She adds that it was too painful for that generation to accept that they were guilty of consent and argues that at the start, the French (and Allied?) soldiers believed in the war, as it was seen to be fighting evil. But she also believes that as it went on, its soldiers became brutalised:

The new way of fighting with cannons and shells, they go so far you don't see what you kill. They do it to you but you don't see yourself do it to them. That brutality is nourished inside you, the violence becomes like a fire inside you.

In pragmatic terms, the troops had to be demobilised and the practicalities of this were as follows. The process had been planned since the middle of the war, when twenty centres were set up. The men were given pay in advance and then the release was begun. Transport and agricultural workers, plus the miners, came first, alongside those over the conscription age and those who were sick or wounded. Each soldier could keep his uniform and helmet and got a suit of clothing or its value in money. If a man did not find work he could claim twenty-four shillings per week for a year, plus an allowance for dependants. As usual, officers were treated differently, as civil service and some education positions (and fees) were reserved for them. By August 1919, over a hundred thousand officers and two and a half million men had been demobilized; unfortunately this still left over a million in uniform. Up and down the country there were protests and marches. Haig, who had received £100,000 as a thank you (he thought this wasn't enough) regarded these movements as being the product of 'the dangerous pacifist types who were tampering with the unity of the army'.

Of particular concern were those who had been wounded. The full disablement pension for a private who was unemployed before the war was set at £71 6s per annum, with extra for dependents. The average manual working wage for male factory employees at that time was £204 15s 9d. An individual who was earning £275 per annum before the war would get £195 each year. Then a sliding scale was set, in which, of course, there were anomalies. The loss of an arm was worth sixteen shillings a week, but two shillings less if the upper part was still in place. A left arm was judged to be worth a shilling less – what the implications were for a left-handed person can only be guessed at. Again, officers fared better, showing that the Edwardian social observations were still in place. A sergeant, for example, was paid two shillings less than his immediate superior and so on up the ranks.

The land where the battles were fought has recovered, but slowly. In his best- selling novel *Birdsong* (on July 1st, 1916, birds were heard singing in the minutes-long gap after the week-long barrage at the Somme ended and before the men went over the top), Sebastian Faulks describes a leisurely afternoon on that eponymous river: 'Berard had been allowed by a friend to moor the boat at the foot of a shady garden and take lunch beneath some apple trees... they slid along beneath the overhanging trees, occasionally coming close to other Sunday pleasure-seekers who called out greetings... a fish broke the surface of the water'.

At the northern end of the Somme, the two mines blown at Hawthorn Ridge (as suggested earlier, the explosion, thrusting and belching black earth into the sky is the iconic piece of footage shown on many TV programmes and was part of Geoffrey Malin's film) have been largely recovered and are now overgrown with thicket. At the southern end of the battlefield the Lochnager crater has defied any attempts of recovery or proposals for re-use. The conflict destroyed nearly one thousand seven hundred settlements and over half a million houses, plus architectural gems such as Ypres Cloth Hall, and the iron harvest, where weapons and munitions still float to the surface every year.

A few years ago I stood on the Butte de Warlencourt, a chalk hill just outside Bapaume, with a good friend of mine. He scraped the earth with his shoe. There were countless small round balls of shrapnel just sitting there. As well as munitions, helmets and other personal possessions, as well as bodies, are still found. Some are unearthed at deliberate excavations such as at Fromelles, described earlier. Many appear as a result of digging and excavation to build roads or house foundations. The latest example I could find, via the Western Front Association website, was a Private William McAleer of the Royal Scots Fusiliers, killed on September 26th 1915 at Loos. He was the only soldier of twenty found that at the time who could be identified.

Sometimes, bodies just rise to the surface. George Nugent, of the Tyneside Scottish, was attacking La Boisselle at the absolute start of the Somme battle when the mine under the ridge near the village was blown at 7.30 am. He may have been buried by the downfall of earth. On 31st October 1998, whilst walking round the crater at the far side from the entrance, Mr Drage of Colchester noticed what he thought might be the remains of a soldier emerging from the chalk. He contacted the Commonwealth War Graves Commission and after relevant approvals had been given the remains were exhumed. They were removed to the CWGC mortuary at Beaurains. They consisted of a human skeleton, the skull of which was broken. Various items of army kit were found, including a rifle, bullets and a water bottle, as well as personal items including a pipe mouthpiece, a silver pen holder and a folding cut-throat razor. The razor had on it the soldier's name and number, and his identity was confirmed by the Newcastle Evening Chronicle. George Nugent was reburied, with military honours, at Ovillers Military Cemetery on 1st July 2000, eighty years after he was killed in battle.

Pitifully, many people turned to spiritualism. Understandably, if a mother, father, wife or sweetheart had lost a dear one they would clutch at straws to contact that person – or his spirit. Traditionally, the Victorian era is seen as the zenith of the spiritualist movement.

After 1916, however, the number of spiritualist societies almost doubled, from a hundred and fifty-eight to over three hundred. This was part of the mass feeling of grief experienced by a large part of society. Arthur Conan Doyle, a genius, although in 1920 he fell for the Cottingley Fairies hoax. He wrote:

'The deaths occurring in almost every family in the land brought a sudden and concentrated interest in the life after death. People not only asked the question, 'If a man die shall he live again?' but they eagerly sought to know if communication was possible with the dear ones they had lost.'

So was Britain different after the war? The answer is a definite yes, with a rider that ten years later some things hadn't changed much at all. The class system had taken a battering. Within the army, and despite reluctance on the part of some of those at the top of the hierarchy, men had been promoted on merit simply because of the decimation of traditionally commissioned officers. This was reflected in society after the war.

Those at the bottom of the socio-economic ladder had benefited. They war had brought full employment and the poor had more money. Economic hard times, however, weren't far away and the Great Depression was only half a generation in the future. Women had clearly won advances – not least the vote (partial, 1918) and some acceptance that they had a different position in the family and society. They smoked, went to the pub and were more independent. Many women lost men in their lives, be they their husbands, brothers, and fathers. Before the war, women mostly depended on men for financial support, but with so many gone to battle and then dying, women had to go to work just to support themselves. The proportion of women in total employment had risen from 24% in July, 1914, to 37% by November 1918. The great landowners had to face a different society but still tried to maintain old privileges. The mass trespass for the 'Right to Roam' at Kinder Scout in 1932 was just one example. Was there a 'Lost Generation', as J B Priestley observed? The answer is in the negative in purely numerical terms as, despite the losses, five and a half million troops came home – about 90% of those who went away (some villages got them all back and were 'Thankful') and the baby bulge of 1919/20 partially rectified this.

If however you were a soldier back from the war missing a limb or with your face deformed, or you were a war widow, you wouldn't be much interested in statistics or figures. I hope the following quote from Plato will at some stage be wrong:

'Only the dead have seen the end of war.'

CHAPTER TEN

LEST WE FORGET

'They shall grow not old, as we that are left grow old.
Age shall not weary them, nor the years condemn.
At the going down of the sun and in the morning
We will remember them'

Laurence Binyon, Red Cross Orderly, The Ode (To The Fallen)

I'd walked past it so many times over so many years, but it was only when I was in my thirties that I really noticed it – that's noticed as in look at and take it in. Over twenty feet wide and a quarter as high, the bronze effect panel at Manchester's Victoria Railway Station is a commemoration of the one thousand four hundred and sixty-five men of the Lancashire and Yorkshire Railway who perished in the Great War. Above it is a tiled wall showing the area covered by the railway company. Unveiled by Douglas Haig, or Earl Haig as he then was, it is just one of over thirty-seven thousand memorials in the UK (there are four and a half times more in France) with around two thousand two hundred and thirty of these being in Wales, one thousand five hundred in Scotland and nearly seven hundred in Northern Ireland. Some are huge, as in Dundee or Cardiff, others, in small villages, parishes or city suburbs, just tablets with a list of names. Then there are the ones in foreign fields

– or deserts, if you include Iraq. All are trying to say 'We will remember'. In Tavistock Place, London, there is one to the conscientious objectors.

Manchester Victoria memorial

The Thiepval
Memorial

The biggest memorial on the old Western Front is at Thiepval on the Somme. This is a memorial to the 'Missing'; those whose remains were never found. The weaponry was such that some soldiers would be blown into many parts or partially vaporised. Others would sink into flooded shell holes or, as at, for example Passchendaele, the mud itself. Many were buried, but then shells blew up the earth they were interred in. In total, on the battlefields of World War One (including the seas), four hundred and sixty-three thousand men were missing from the Allies side.

The Thiepval memorial was designed by Sir Edwin Lutyens, whose other works include the Cenotaph and Liverpool Metropolitan (Catholic) Cathedral. Looking like a huge upturned magnet, it was built in red brick and Portland stone between 1928 and 1932. The original has been resurfaced with Accrington brick, beautifully appropriate as the Pals from that mid-Lancashire town fought at the northern end of the battlefield. The names of the seventy-two thousand one hundred and ninety-four men missing in action on the battlefield of the Somme are inscribed on sixty-four huge stone panels. These form each of four faces of a total of sixteen piers for the building. The memorial is located on a high ridge of ground and the top of it can be clearly seen from many places on the battlefield. It was this vantage point that gave the Germans such an advantage in 1916. Its foundations are nearly six metres in depth and they had to be so strong as they sit on ground which was extensively tunnelled in the war. Two hundred thousand people visit here each year.

The memorial has the following inscription: 'Here are recorded names of officers and men of the British Armies who fell on the Somme battlefields between July 1915 and March 1918 but to whom the fortune of war denied the known and honoured burial given to their comrades in death'.

The remains of a number of men whose names are on the memorial have been found since it was built, but the decision was taken not to erase these soldiers' names. Technically, that contradicts the meaning or rationale of the memorial; emotionally, it has to be the correct decision.

The memorial below is a typically British church domestic one. I show it because the name of the author's great uncle, Benjamin Brooks, is on it.

St Stephen and All Martyrs, Lever Bridge, Bolton

There are sometimes anomalies on memorials. Lord Leverhulme, founder of the Lever Brothers corporation in the last quarter of the nineteenth century, built a model workers' village on the Wirral in 1888. It is a quite lovely place and should have been the template for other industrialists, in more ways than one. Its war memorial was designed and sculpted by Leverhulme's friend, Goscombe John, one of the 'New Sculptors'. Unveiled by Sergeant E G Eames (who was blinded at the Somme) and Private R E Cruickshank on the 3rd of December 1921, it sits on a huge, circular plinth in the heart of the village, and honours those of Lord Leverhulme's employees who fell in the Great War, as well as remembering the different services that supported them. In most ways it is magnificent and appropriate. The one fault is that it carries an inscription that ends:

> DULCE ET DECORUM
> EST PRO PATRIA MORI
> THEIR NAME
> SHALL REMAIN
> FOR EVER AND
> THEIR GLORY
> SHALL NOT BE
> BLOTTED OUT.

Where is the anomaly? 'DULCE ET DECORUM EST PRO PATRIA MORI' does not appear to fit correctly at all. It is translated as 'It is sweet and fitting/honourable to die for one's country,' and is from Horace. It is a cry to take up arms. In fact, though used by others in the Great War, it is so well known because of Wilfrid Owen's famous poem, in which it is used with great irony:

> *My friend, you would not tell with such high zest,*
> *To children ardent for some desperate glory,*
> *The old Lie;*
> *Dulce et Decorum est Pro Patria Mori.*

I think Owen would have pointed to the penultimate line – 'The old Lie' - as the crux of the poem. His death a week before the Armistice seems to confirm the point.

Other towns were so devastated that they were slow to put up any form of remembrance. Neilston, six or seven miles to the south west of Glasgow, lost sixteen men on one September day at the Somme and nearly another one hundred and fifty in the conflict as a whole. The small town was too shocked and traumatised to build a memorial; only now is one being constructed. Sadly, not all memorials are cherished by all people. Perhaps we can cite ignorance.

Barr Memorial after the theft of copper

In the winter of 1921, The War Office handed over responsibility for British cemeteries to the Imperial War Graves Commission, the 'Imperial' becoming 'Commonwealth' in 1960. The following are from the Commonwealth War Graves Commission's website. The Commission cares for the graves and memorials of almost one million seven hundred thousand Commonwealth servicemen and women who died in the two world wars. Over the years, the original crosses were replaced by tablets or gravestones carrying the individual's name, rank (of course), regimental badge and date of death, or the motto 'known unto God'. They became what Kipling called 'The Silent Cities', and originally they were tended by more than five hundred gardeners, mainly ex-soldiers. The names of almost seven hundred and sixty thousand people can be found on memorials to the missing. The largest Commission cemetery in the world is Tyne Cot in Belgium and the cemetery at Etaples is the largest in France. All Americans whose remains were intact were repatriated.

Those figures sometimes tell a full story but sometimes do what statistics can do – bewilder the reader. Here is a true story that does what this book strives to achieve – the encapsulation of a much bigger narrative by exploring a smaller, representative part. The people concerned are relatives of relatives. In 1980, in the small Lancashire town of Farnworth, near Bolton, Martha Ellen Chapman passed away. She was the grandmother of Mike Chapman, and was married to Thomas Albert Chapman. Her son, Mike's father, was also Thomas Albert. When Mike and his wife Bernadette were clearing up Martha's possessions they came across a small paper giving information about Thomas senior's death in World War One and his place of burial; a graveyard in Anneux near Cambrai. It's in the Nord department of north-east France. By coincidence Thomas had joined the King's Own Regiment, of which many Arkholme, Nether Kellet and Over Kellet men had been part.

The Chapmans decided on a visit to Anneux and at the cemetery they and their daughters, Helen and Laura, took a row of gravestones each. It was Laura who spotted her great grandfather's headstone first. Eighteen months or so later the family made the pilgrimage again, this time with Mike's dad, Albert junior, in tow; though he had been in the RAF in the Second War it was the first time he'd been out of the country. Thomas Albert senior had joined up in 1916 and been wounded twice, returning to his home to recuperate. On his third time back in France he was killed, five weeks before the Armistice. His son saw his father's grave for the first time sixty-five years later, in 1983. He cannot remember seeing his father alive.

The most poignant burial/memorial is probably that to the unknown warrior. In the dark of the night of Sunday November 7th, 1920, half a dozen bodies were exhumed from graves in north east France and Belgium, all British and all unidentified. Wrapped in Union Jacks, they were laid in the chapel of St Pol, a small town between Béthune and Arras. Haig's successor, Brigadier General L J Wyatt, selected one at random and the body was taken back to Britain on HMS *Verdun* and on November 11th, the soldier was buried in Westminster Abbey. Six horses, repatriated from the Western Front, pulled the carriage.

Over the following week over a million people visited the site. The inscription on the tomb reads: 'They buried him among the kings, because he had done good toward God and toward his house'. That body could be one of your ancestors.

Historian Peter Barton, last referred to in Chapter Three, has done something that might help name many of those who at the moment are 'unknown'. He has discovered an archive in the basement of the Red Cross headquarters in Geneva, virtually untouched since 1918. The organisation knew it had a vast amount of information there, but Mr Barton is the first to study it in detail. It documents information about the death, burial or capture of more than twenty million soldiers from thirty countries who took part in the Great War. Barton stumbled across the records after being commissioned by the Australian government to find the identities of soldiers found at Pheasant Wood, Fromelles, France (see Chapter Three).

The trail led him to the Red Cross Museum in Geneva, where he was given access to their basement and the records kept there.

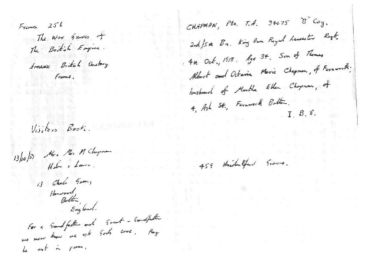

Visitors' Book, Anneux Cemetery

These were passed to the Red Cross by the combatant countries at the end of the war, as the organisation was acting as a go-between for the protagonists. Information was then copied and passed to the soldiers' home countries, but, according to Mr Barton, the UK's copy of the data no longer exists, much of it having been destroyed in the Second World War. The same fate is believed to have befallen the records in France and Germany. The Red Cross is already working to bring the archive into the computer age. The organisation has set aside £2.4 million to conserve and digitise the paper records. 'We want to archive these records because it will be far easier for families to access the information they require,' said a Red Cross spokesman. Let's hope it reveals a few more Thomas Albert Chapmans.

The National Memorial Arboretum near the village of Alrewas, north of Lichfield, is a quite remarkable place. Set in a hundred and fifty acres of parkland, lawns and woodland, it features memorials to the military and civilians alike. The most touching is probably that to those who were executed while in service. Called 'Shot at Dawn', it is one of the first of the tributes to catch the rising sun. The arboretum is well worth a visit, and the scones are delicious.

The criteria for a medal for involvement in the First World War could be applied to a 'Thankful' village, in that the individual concerned should have gone to a 'foreign field' – and in the case of 'Thankful', returned. There were three basic medals for those whom had fought. The most commonly granted was the British War Medal, of which over six and a half million were minted. This was, basically, given to any member of the fighting forces who had left his or her native shore in any part of the British Empire while on service; it did not matter whether he/she entered a theatre of war or not. It is silver and circular, and carries an image of the head of King George V on one side with a depiction of Saint George on the other. There is a straight clasp and the ribbon is mainly gold with three stripes of white, black and blue on either side.

The second is the Victory Medal. This was awarded to anyone who had been in a theatre of war, so all those who, for example, were on the Western Front, Mesopotamia or Italy would be eligible. Those stationed in an area that saw no fighting would not qualify. By definition, all who got the Victory Medal therefore also got the British War Medal. Again, this can guide us as to whether an individual should be on a war scroll as a 'Returner' or not. It is made of bronze with a depiction of the Greek Goddess of Victory on one side. On the other is inscribed 'The Great War for Civilisation'. The ribbon is almost like a spectrum of colours. Five and three quarter million were issued.

The 1914 Star was awarded to those who had fought in the very earliest stages of the war in Belgium or France, and is hence known as the 'Mons Star'; an alternative is the 1914-15 Star for those who fought in any theatre of war before the end of December, 1915, but did not receive the 1914 Star. As the name suggests, they are stellar in shape and carried the individual's number and regiment on the reverse. Over two million were issued.

A person who had all three medals was said to have 'Pip, Squeak and Wilfred', named after three Daily Mirror cartoon characters. Holding the two later ones, the War Medal and the Victory Medal, gave the person a 'Mutt and Jeff', again, two cartoon creations.

Ever done something that was 'a bit over the top'? Do you like to 'chat' or 'chew the fat'? Like things a bit 'cushy'? All these words or phrases were popularised in World War One and then brought back to Britain. How many times have you heard a sportsman or entertainer talking about something as 'being worse than the Somme'? The only thing I can think of is Passchendaele. Lots of sayings have drifted down to us from the war, though, and are in use without the person using them knowing the origin. Chats were lice and the removal of them while talking to a colleague became a 'chat', though some sources say it was already in common usage. Hopefully, 'At the eleventh hour' is self-explanatory; if not, Chapter Nine should explain.

A number of charities for ex-servicemen were formed in the early years of the nineteenth century. The Great War saw the development of many others, of which the best known is probably the Royal British Legion. This evolved from the merger of four almost rival organisations, all having strong political affiliations, the earliest being the National Association of Discharged Sailors and Soldiers, formed in the north of England in 1916. In 1921, the four sank their political differences and pooled their resources and formed the British Legion, of which Earl Haig became President. The 'Legion' offers care and companionship, fights pension claims and generally promotes the welfare of present and previous members of the Armed Services. Its biggest event is Poppy Day.

In passing, the author feels he should comment on the wearing of poppies, which seem to be developing into a fashion accessory worn earlier and earlier in the days before November 11th by presenters and the like. Not approved!

So we have Thankful Villages, Doubly Thankful ones and those who are not so thankful. There will always be a problem with what a Thankful Village really is and there's no official definition of course. 'Where the men went away and came back.' Went away where? Training in the next town? The other side of the world? I think the individual should have been on foreign soil, as defined by the criteria for a British War Medal, which in Arkholme's case rules out two men at least. Even so, it IS still a Thankful Village; the relevant men just shouldn't be included as Returners. And too much delving into such definitions makes the author feel uncomfortable; the main idea of this book is to tell what was, predominantly, an awful time for most people in Britain via the medium of three villages, not to conduct a semantic investigation of their lives.

There are villages and communities that are the opposite of Thankful Villages, in that they were particularly hard hit by the war, such as Neilston, above. As mentioned earlier in relation to the Accrington Pals, the idea of those Chums battalions was sound, except when it came to deaths. On line is a photograph of the Edinburgh Academy in 1904-05. There are sixteen faces looking out; bright, expectant, optimistic, a life ahead. Only eight survived the war. The epithet 'The bravest little street in England' was given to Chapel Street in Altrincham, which provided a hundred and sixty-one men for the war effort from a total of sixty dwellings. One hundred and thirty-two got back in one piece. In his book *No Thankful Village,* Chris Howell depicts the effect the war had on the community where he was brought up in around Radstock and

Midsomer Norton in Somerset. A mining area, it felt the events of the war as well as those of the early twenties and 1926. The testimonies are typical and reflect those described in this book.

To show the absurdities of war and its propaganda, let us finish with a quote from his book. He cites Janet Flagg, talking about her father, the appropriately named Tommy Atkins (all British infantrymen were 'Tommies' after the name Tommy Atkins was used as an example in a soldier's pay book in the Napoleonic Wars):

When the war ended, Dad went on into Germany for a while, until they'd got things sorted out. He learned to speak the language and said time and time again how much he liked the German people – people who had been trying to kill him! Preferred them to English, he said.

So we started this book with a village with no war memorial, but a scroll in a church, another with an embossed plaque, and a third with a worthy, truncated war memorial and ten names. The author has tried to show how ninety lives from these villages represented millions.

For the Returners, it is just a shame that the Great War did not become the 'War to End All Wars', and that Britain did not, after all, turn out to be the promised 'Land Fit for Heroes'.

Printed in Great Britain
by Amazon